Transformative Doctoral Rese
Professionals

CRITICAL ISSUES IN THE FUTURE OF LEARNING AND TEACHING

Volume 12

Series Editors:

Britt-Marie Apelgren, *University of Gothenburg, Sweden*
Pamela Burnard, *University of Cambridge, UK*
Nese Cabaroglu, *University of Cukurova, Turkey*
Pamela M. Denicolo, *University of Surrey, UK*
Nicola Simmons, *Brock University, Canada*

Founding Editor:

Michael Kompf† (Brock University, Canada)

Scope:

This series represents a forum for important issues that do and will affect how learning and teaching are thought about and practised. All educational venues and situations are undergoing change because of information and communications technology, globalization and paradigmatic shifts in determining what knowledge is valued. Our scope includes matters in primary, secondary and tertiary education as well as community-based informal circumstances. Important and significant differences between information and knowledge represent a departure from traditional educational offerings heightening the need for further and deeper understanding of the implications such opportunities have for influencing what happens in schools, colleges and universities around the globe. An inclusive approach helps attend to important current and future issues related to learners, teachers and the variety of cultures and venues in which educational efforts occur. We invite forward-looking contributions that reflect an international comparative perspective illustrating similarities and differences in situations, problems, solutions and outcomes.

Transformative Doctoral Research Practices for Professionals

Edited by

Pamela Burnard, Tatjana Dragovic, Julia Flutter and Julie Alderton
University of Cambridge, UK

SENSE PUBLISHERS
ROTTERDAM/BOSTON/TAIPEI

A C.I.P. record for this book is available from the Library of Congress.

ISBN: 978-94-6300-628-6 (paperback)
ISBN: 978-94-6300-629-3 (hardback)
ISBN: 978-94-6300-630-9 (e-book)

Published by: Sense Publishers,
P.O. Box 21858,
3001 AW Rotterdam,
The Netherlands
https://www.sensepublishers.com/

All chapters in this book have undergone peer review.

Printed on acid-free paper

TABLE OF CONTENTS

Part 3: Generating Impact

Conclusion

PREFACE

Being a researcher is a challenge. Being a professional practitioner in education is a challenge. The idea of being a professional who bridges both practice and research describes well someone who is doing a professional education doctorate; an even greater challenge, which has been largely under-represented and under-theorised in higher education globally.

Who elects to do a professional education doctorate or doctorate of education? Professionals who are practitioners – that is, those who 'practice and develop expertise' ('do it') in a profession and wish to become researchers or scholars who 'study it' and conduct research. The researching professional is a hybrid category of those who 'do it' and 'study it' simultaneously. Professionals who elect to do a professional (education) doctorate differ from those who elect to a part-time PhD because they may not be researching their own practice.

Among the many problems with which doctoral communities must grapple is the practical dynamics of what makes professional education doctorates really worth doing. When do people feel most empowered, engaged, and creative? When do both new and established doctoral researchers, and their supervisors and lecturers, feel most challenged and stimulated: when doing research or when supporting or teaching students working on professional doctorates?

The initiative for a book on *Transformative Doctoral Research Practices for Professionals*, encompassing a variety of different viewpoints, from students to lecturers, supervisors and course managers, arises from a need for critical insight into the doing, supporting, teaching and learning of doctoral research.

The purpose of this edited volume is, primarily, to explore the distinct research practices and unique journeying of professional practitioner-researchers and their supervisors and lecturers who stand at the centre of doctoral education. While the topics feature critical issues that characterize professional doctorates, the ways in which these scholars have chosen to address their journeying illustrate the diversity of voices in practice, with project examples from within and beyond educational settings.

This volume offers the first institutional-specific[1] collection in the form of a collaboratively authored volume, with the purpose and goal of sharing the lived-through debates, deliberations, challenges and experiences of a group of professional doctoral students, their supervisors and lecturers. This book is designed to help professional doctoral students and their supervisors and educators understand what doctoral education means in contemporary practice and to reflect on, address and integrate, an understanding of the practical and theoretical issues involved in journeying as a doctoral student. It provides a valuable showcase of key themes and contemporary issues as experienced by a diversity of voices in an international community of professional doctoral students and their educators whose voices will relate to an international audience. This group of doctoral students draws from diverse disciplines which include education, business, veterinary science, physiotherapy, and counselling.

The book showcases the mapping of professional practices at different phases and stages of a five year doctoral journey, the imperative of reflexivity as one moves from practitioner to researching professional and scholar identities, and the placing of 'practice' at the centre of doctorates. Within the scenario of one institution, the aims of the volume can be articulated as questions, such as: What does it mean to be a doctoral researcher and what practices are of central concern to the critical reflexivity and positioning involved with the outer and inner journeys it engenders? Why and how do writing practices challenge and delight doctoral researchers, supervisors and doctoral educators engaged in creating and supporting the development of innovative portfolio doctorates? And what is their notion of a 'professional' doctorate and 'doctorateness'? When do studies make a ripple and/or a splash? How do we think about and address crucial issues surrounding the outcomes and impact of our research? How does theorising practice play a role in the creation of a new professional identity (of a researching professional) and in the journeying of a professional doctoral researcher, supervisor and doctorate educator and how do professional doctorates represent, facilitate and generate impact on practice and participation within and across disciplinary and institutional structures and practices?

The aim of this book, therefore, is to engage and explore some of the critical issues for doctoral students and educators in the teaching and learning of professional doctoral journeying. The voices of novice researchers, as well as developing and established researchers, are put together to create, in their own right, a rationale for why professional doctoral research matters. The manner in which the book has been compiled will give doctoral educators and students an innovative and appealing way of deliberating on the diverse paths and critical issues arising in professional doctoral research which reform and transform professional practice. The contributions highlight the latest theories and research approaches which have been developed in practice.

The book is divided into three main parts: Part 1 'Mapping doctoral practices', Part 2 'Theorising doctoral journeying', and Part 3 'Generating impact'.

The poem that follows is offered as a way of thanking every author who shared their journeying, their voices and their research with us, the readers. It is also an expression of (and site for disturbance of the usual way of being and becoming, thinking and doing, teaching and learning), what it is to be a professional researcher. Sometimes it's just not enough to talk or reflect, read or write in conventional forms about the rich and fruitful experience of doctoral work.

I encourage all doctoral educators and students who read this book to embrace the question and issues raised within *Transformative Doctoral Research Practices for Professionals* and to maybe rethink the role that writing has in your practice, and how it is represented in doctoral education and in research.

The Reflexive Researching Professional by Pamela Burnard

We talk, we reflect, we think, we share the individual account
How this or that
rap or rhythm, practice or perception, article or chapter
moves us
We do. We study. We theorize the ripples that change us
How *personal* the *practice*;
How professional practice *is* personal
Reflecting on the person, the *profession*, the *researching* professional
Doing a professional doctorate
How practice is reflective yet may not be reflexive
How practice can be research or practice *as* research
Playing with and reflecting on ideas, opinions, assumptions and experiences,
Documenting, representing, seeing and *re*-seeing and unpacking practices with new
Sight, in-sight into words, images, metaphors
Reflecting on the unspoken
Articulating the taken-for-granted
Reflexively fighting familiarity
Doing and theorizing research
Doing research, as researching professionals
Into the night
Doing research, writing our selves
Without silencing voices
Theorizing professional lives
Writing our selves in *re*-search

Pamela Burnard

NOTE

[1] University of Cambridge, Faculty of Education, Doctor of Education programme (see http://www.educ.cam.ac.uk/courses/graduate/doctoral/edd/)

ACKNOWLEDGEMENTS

We would like to thank all of our contributing authors for their work, their willingness to attend to detail, and their generosity in sharing their professional doctoral journeying and examples of practice. We would also like to thank the team at Sense Publishers, in particular Michel Lokhorst (Sense Publishers Director), Jolanda Karada (Sense Publishers Production Coordinator) and Series Editors Pamela Denicolo, Nicola Simmons, Britt-Marie Apelgren and Nese Cabaroglu for their support and advice. Thanks are due to our friends, families and colleagues for their support and encouragement, and especially to the EdD cohort for our initial and ongoing discussions and reflections on doctoral journeying as professionals which stimulated the idea for the book. We gratefully acknowledge support from the EdD supervisors and advisors along with the Faculty of Education, University of Cambridge (who funds the annual EdD one-day-conference) which featured some of the themes shared in this volume. The front cover's image, 'Water drop close-up', was retrieved from the public domain stock photograph website Skitterphoto (http://skitterphoto.com/?portfolio=water-drop-close-up), accessed on 19 May 2016. We also thank David Litchfield (www.davidlitchfieldillustration.com), an illustrator from Bedfordshire in the UK, for the particular colouring of the cover design. The idea of the cover's metaphor of water expresses the flow of ideas and the fluidity in identity experienced by our contributors in their lives as researching professionals; the ripples emanating from the droplet remind us of the circles of influence which emerge through their work, expanding outwards towards, as yet, unknown destinations. We hope that this volume provides a source of inspiration and ideas for all those who work in doctoral education and that it may stimulate a deeper consideration of what constitutes doctorate journeying for professionals all over the world and how this innovative form of knowledge creation can contribute to future global needs.

LIST OF ILLUSTRATIONS

FIGURES

TABLES

INTRODUCTION

JULIA FLUTTER

1. FIELDS AND OCEANS

Helping Professional Doctorate Students to Orientate Themselves and
Navigate through Their Practitioner Research Journeys

INTRODUCTION

In academic research we often find reference to the phrase 'fields of enquiry', particularly in the discourse of social and educational domains, and this agricultural metaphor is sustained in terms used for the various processes and tools used to investigate social worlds. Social researchers talk, for example, about 'entering the field' and 'gathering' data as if venturing into the world to harvest material for processing (analysis) before its eventual distribution and consumption by a society hungrily seeking new information to build up its body of knowledge and increase its capacities for growth and improvement. However, for the beginning professional doctorate student, the journey they are about to embark on will feel much more fluid and uncertain than being on dry land; the initial expanse of ideas and challenges can be as daunting as an ocean spreading out to an unclear horizon.

This chapter offers a starting point – a chart or map – for the discussions which follow throughout the book concerning the unsettling voyages of professional doctoral researchers, and a set of 'cardinal points' are identified to enable professional doctoral students, and those who work with them on their research journeys, to orientate themselves and navigate successfully through to their chosen destinations. In adopting the metaphor of a voyage we are nonetheless mindful of its potential limitations and concur with Hughes and Tight's warning that "[t]he predominance of a single narrative structure" for discussing professional doctorate students' experiences should be, "treated with caution lest it becomes a hegemonic lens through which all experience is to be understood" (2013, p. 765).

Moreover, the word 'field' itself bears a specific connotation in social theory, particularly in the influential work of the French social theorist, Pierre Bourdieu. Under Bourdieu's definition the notion of 'field' is used to represent a network, social structure or set of relationships and it may be based on educational, religious, cultural, institutional or other kinds of social collectiveness (Navarro, 2006). His theory proposes that people are likely to experience power differently depending on the field in which they find themselves at a given point in time and thus Bourdieu's theoretical framework has strongly resonating implications for those engaged in professional doctorate programmes, which can be seen to represent an overlapping

P. Burnard et al. (Eds.), Transformative Doctoral Research Practices for Professionals, 3–12.

intersection of the two distinctive fields of professional practice and academic research. Bourdieu's theory attempts to explain the tensions and contradictions arising when people find themselves engaged in different fields (the workplace, the home, university and so on) and are challenged by these varying social arenas each exerting its own particular influence on an individual's power and agency (Bourdieu, 1980, 1984). In the chapters which follow we will explore how professional doctoral programmes give rise to tensions and contradictions, and what impact this may have on what Bourdieu called 'habitus', the socialized norms or tendencies which guide behaviour and thinking.

Before setting off on our voyage we need to consider why professional practitioners have chosen to take up the challenge of doctoral research in the first place, with all its inherent risks, burdens and uncertainties. Becoming an established professional within a particular field is rightly considered as being a significant achievement and the demands of practice may result in long working hours with little opportunity for continuing professional development or even a personal life beyond the workplace, so what could prompt a professional practitioner to set aside the precious commodities of their limited time and energy to take up professional doctoral study? The answers to that question are neither simple nor generalizable: however, it is a thread of discussion which will be woven throughout this book and we will return to it in the concluding section in the light of the contributions by our professional doctoral student authors. Wellington points out that for some the rationale is largely pragmatic: "Those already working might see it as career development or continuing professional development; or it might be seen as a way of researching one's own practice, with a view to improving it..." (Wellington, 2013, p. 1492). For others, however, the reasons are more complex and multi-faceted. For the time being we should content ourselves with noting that, whatever the reasons for their voyage into the unknown, professional doctoral students share common ground insofar as they commit to undertaking research within their own professional settings and practice on a part-time basis and represent a wide diversity of professions, contexts and cultures. This book includes contributions from professional doctorate researchers representing education, medical practice, counseling and business administration, but, internationally, professional doctorate programmes have drawn students from a wide diversity of professions including domains as diverse as law, engineering, architecture, nursing, veterinary medicine and business management (Flint & Costley, 2010). Our intrepid voyagers enter the academic ocean from differing starting points and the ontological and epistemological foundations upon which these 'home ports' rest are likely to exert a powerful influence on their thinking as researchers. What constitutes 'knowledge' in a professional domain like counselling, for example, may be derived from an interpretivist epistemology where knowledge is regarded as being subjective and fluid; in 'technical' professions knowledge claims are more likely to be anchored within the objective post-positivist paradigm. The diversity in students' starting points has a significant role to play, not only in shaping the professional doctorate student's own experiences and professional development, but also in signaling the wider, societal potential of the professional doctorate as a catalyst for transformative change. This point is exemplified in Piercy and Gordon's study of a multi-professional doctoral programme at Sheffield Hallam University (England) which draws students from health, social care, sport and biomedicine, where it is noted that, "students commented on their exposure to new worldviews and research contexts through the rich mix of professions represented in the cohorts. Even for those accustomed to multi-professional learning, this mix was considerably greater than they had previously experienced" (2015, p. 395). Once again, this is an idea that we shall leave as a placeholder and return to consider and examine its significance in greater depth during our concluding chapter.

Here we begin our voyage with an overview of the themes which characterize the professional doctorate experience but this is not intended as a timeline or a step-by-step guide, nor, in keeping with our maritime metaphor, is it to be regarded as a navigation chart to aid an inexperienced traveler. The themes outlined below represent distinctive and significant facets of the professional doctoral programme as experienced by students and those who work with them. Each of these themes will be found within the individual narratives contained in this book, although how they are manifested within each narrative differs widely: in some accounts a particular theme may be foregrounded as being particularly important or challenging, whilst for others there may be a balance in the salience afforded to each sequence. The five 'cardinal themes' are as follows:

- *Embarkation* is a theme which denotes the experiences involved in setting out on the professional doctoral journey and includes both affective aspects – the hopes and aspirations; the excitements, fears and uncertainties; and pragmatic aspects – the planning, decision-making and preparations required. Recognizing embarkation as a moment of leave-taking as well as of entering new circumstances, our exploration of this process attempts to capture the dilemmas, opportunities and changes integral to the process.

- *Learning the ropes* explores the development of new skills, capacities and identity as students travel through the course of their research. It is argued that this experience has some similarities to a form of apprenticeship, but for the professional doctorate student who has extensive expertise within their own profession, it is a process that involves a complex re-shifting of identity and power that sets it apart from simple models of apprenticeship learning.

- *Guiding lights* is a somewhat nebulous theme that embraces the influences which shape and support the student's journeying and includes associates (university staff, workplace colleagues, fellow students, families and friends), professional and academic figures that provide inspiration and stimulating thought, and resources needed in moments of crisis.

- *Logging the journey* refers to processes through which the student's doctoral journey is documented, and includes consideration of the experiences involved in writing, dissemination and final assessment of the research. Writing can be experienced as one of the most challenging aspects of the doctoral journey for many students and the student contributors to this book provide some insightful reflections on their growth as authors.

- *New waters* represents, appropriately, a more fluid theme which is used to denote the students' arrivals at their destinations, both anticipated and intentional, or sometimes unintended and wholly unexpected. For some students a sense of 'having arrived' begins long before their dissertation or portfolio is completed as they become aware of profound changes in their identities, professional practice or personal outlook resulting from their doctoral studies.

EMBARKATION

There is a well-known and often-quoted line – often attributed to an ancient Chinese philosopher named Lao Tzu (Laozi) – which states, "The journey of a thousand miles begins with a single step". The singular, life-changing moment when the decision is made to embark on a professional doctorate, however, is likely to represent the nexus of many previous journeys in the academic, professional and personal life of the student and it may be difficult to identify the first step on this new journey. The decision to take up a professional doctorate may have been motivated by one reason or an interplay of different reasons, and could be the result of affective or pragmatic considerations: it may have been reached in a brief moment of decisiveness or be the result of months, or even years, of deliberation and wavering uncertainty. What sets the professional doctorate student apart from most other postgraduate students is their commitment to continued engagement with their professional practice during the course of their research and this adds a further layer of complexity to the decision-making process at the outset. Pragmatic questions are likely to arise for the student, their workplace institution and colleagues, and the higher education institution about manageability with regard to personal, financial, professional and academic requirements. Decisions need to be made on the student's time management, how access to resources will be provided and who will be responsible for the course fees and research costs. On a deeper level, questions also emerge about what is intended to be gained through the research: what outcome and forms of impact are expected for the individual student, their workplace and profession and for society at large? For those supporting the student at this vital stage, it is important to identify ways of providing clear answers to these questions and concerns and to offer appropriate structures through which to access guidance that enables applicants to make informed decisions. Listening to professional doctorate students' perspectives on their experiences of embarking on their research journeys provides a valuable source of evidence, enabling us to cross-examine them as 'expert witnesses' on teaching and learning (Rudduck & McIntyre, 2007) and to discover from these first-hand accounts what helps, and what may hinder, them as they make their way into the world of academic research.

Clearly, the initial commitment to enrolling on a professional doctorate programme brings with it a raft of further decisions, preparations and questions and, as we will be seeing in the chapters which follow, casting off into this new venture will necessarily involve change and, perhaps more surprisingly, a sense of leave-taking and even loss for some students. However confident and experienced the professional doctorate student may be within their professional context or how comfortable they feel within the hallowed halls of academia, accepting an enrolment on a professional doctorate programme is a decision that may bring in its wake unforeseen challenges and, as our students' stories vividly demonstrate, its implications can extend far beyond the immediate horizons envisaged at the outset. For those students who are joining a doctoral programme from overseas, these challenges are likely to be magnified and the arrival in a new cultural setting will add a further layer of complexity to their needs, as Burton and Kirshbaum point out:

> There are many factors that create an impact on the specialized and diverse group of international students. Wellington and Sikes (2006) suggest that doctoral students present with wide-ranging academic, personal and professional needs. This is very pertinent as regards the characteristics of international Professional Doctoral students whose professional priorities and assumptions on which they operate may differ substantially from those of their international counterparts in similar professions. In addition, studying in a second language, which is often the case, and in a different cultural context or socio-cultural climate, presents complex situations for the international student and their teaching/supervisory teams. (2013, p. 112)

Enabling students to cope with these new demands, wherever they originate from, is a paramount concern and we now turn to consider the other sequences which help them navigate their way through the professional doctoral course.

LEARNING THE ROPES

Engaging in, and with, research requires specialist knowledge and ways of thinking which may be far removed from the professional context with which a professional doctorate student is familiar. The expert practitioner with an established professional standing may feel disconcerted by the acquisition of a new identity as an uninitiated research 'novice' and it will necessarily take time and effort for the student to become familiar with the practices of academic knowledge creation. Whilst it may be a relatively straightforward learning process for a professional doctorate student to develop a firm grounding of knowledge and understanding of research methodology, and to acquire specialist language and skills for engaging with complex ideas and academic argument – the attempt to intertwine professional and academic domains often gives rise to tensions which can make learning the 'ropes', and how to bind these new strands to the established professional ones, a much more problematic and demanding task. Again it is important to note that for international students these issues are compounded by being set within a linguistic and cultural environment which is unfamiliar. Ryan and Viete (2013), discussing postgraduate provision in the Australian higher education context, argue for the adoption of the following principles:

> ...we suggest that not only policy, but also curriculum, assessment, the educational community, and teaching and learning practices should all reflect the following principles:
>
> 1. That diversity be valued. This requires a less normative and more positive valuing of different ways of knowing and communicating knowledge. It also requires that having diverse linguistic resources be recognised and valued.
>
> 2. That interactions be respectful. This requires explicit attention to providing equitable opportunities for knowledge and ideas to be explored by teachers and students, and not only on the terms of the host community. It requires all communicators, not just a few to actively search for meaning in what others say and write. It also requires support for communicators and regulation of non-inclusive behaviour.
>
> 3. That there be a focus on growth. This prohibits the deficit view, and takes pains to acknowledge achievement. (2013, p. 311)

The learning process is also sustained throughout the course of the doctoral journey, although the nature of what is being learnt, and how, is liable to change in relation to the stage at which the research is: for example, in the writing up phase, skills for communicating the study's execution, its findings and eventual outcomes will place specific demands on a student's capabilities which may be wholly new or require substantial adaption in the face of stringent, academic criteria. Learning the ropes for a lengthy, doctoral voyage therefore requires an extensive, sustained receptiveness to new ideas and ways of thinking, as well as the ability to acquire new capacities and adjust existing skillsets. It is also important to recognize that embracing new ideas, skills and ways of thinking may involve shifts in power relationships, particularly within the professional context of the workplace (Flint & Barnard, 2010).

We will see how students are grappling with mastery of the ropes in the chapters which follow and their stories show that, for some, attempting to hold the strands of research and professional practice together has brought unexpected challenges, whilst for others it is opening new possibilities as they discover that binding together the strands of research and practice can lend strength to both.

GUIDING LIGHTS

Our cardinal points described so far are focused on the individual student because, to a large extent, the research voyage is an independent venture and the decision to set out on it and to engage with a 'new world' is experienced as a personal choice. However, it is important to understand how other people contribute to the student's journeying, whether they are guiding the professional doctoral student's course or providing companionship, critical friendship and emotional support. At times of stress, these guiding lights are likely to be perceived as beacons in the darkness and, as our student stories illustrate, a supervisor's words or a colleague's advice given at a moment of stress and confusion can prove pivotal, rescuing their research from heading in the wrong direction, which would result in a considerable waste of time and effort, or even being abandoned on the rocks of despair as the student sinks under the weight of coping with multiple demands. The significance of such support should not be underestimated, as the stories which follow will demonstrate, and it is important that those providing professional doctoral programmes or working with students in their professional contexts recognize the need to provide opportunities for students to build supportive relationships and be able to find the right sources of guidance and help as, and when, they need them. The supervisor will be likely to occupy the central position in a student's journey and therefore much rides on the effectiveness of this working relationship. How the interaction between supervisor and researcher operates to shape the doctoral journey will be unique to each research journey; however, as we shall see, there are some common features evident in the narratives of the students and supervisors in this book which suggest the kinds of features that may characterize a successful supervisory experience. As Burton and Kishbaum (2013) suggest, it is vital that relationships between the supervisor and student are dialogic in nature and, on a broader plain, the collegiality of staff and student peers should provide a learning environment where all voices are respected and valued and creative confidence is nurtured. Moreover, the characteristic of work-based doctorates as being essentially "structured through objectives that are identified by the candidate as central to his or her practice" (Costley & Lester, 2012, p. 260) positions the student in a rather different relationship to the doctoral programme compared with traditional doctoral studies:

> The essential principles of the work-based doctorate are that it uses the candidate's experience and context as a starting point; it encourages reflection on and articulation of previous learning and achievement as a basis from which to take forward the doctoral endeavour. (Costley & Lester, 2012, p. 261)

Although doctoral study is independent, the collegiality and support afforded by fellow travelers on the professional doctorate journey is also important to take into account, particularly as many programmes are multi-professional and therefore bring together a mix of differing professions. Working in parallel rather than in collaboration, professional doctoral students are likely to draw social and emotional support from their peers and benefit from opportunities to learn from others' professional domains in a form of cross-pollination across fields that sometimes only rarely come into contact with each other. Piercy and Gordon (2015) describe the professional doctoral students' experiences in their study as "travelling alone together" and they argue that the student cohort helps to combat feelings of isolation which can lead to non-completion.

LOGGING THE JOURNEY

A ship's log records every significant detail of a voyage but writing an account of the professional doctorate differs in several key respects. Firstly, the details of the research journey are likely to be recorded informally in a research journal which is not intended as a public account, and remains the personal repository of material that the researcher wishes to keep for future reference or simply as a keepsake. Secondly, the public account of the research journey will initially take the form of a thesis or portfolio which will be subjected to evaluative scrutiny by an expert audience, and subsequently its findings may be disseminated in publications, articles, books and conference papers. It may also be used to provide guidance for practitioners as an institutional planning document, or its recommendations may even extend to public policymaking arenas. Far from being a simple 'log' of what the student has accomplished during their voyage, the thesis or portfolio represents the culmination of the doctoral study and will present their learning, thinking and discovering as a formal submission for assessment at the highest academic level. In addition, the student is generally required to defend their work in a face-to-face evaluation (such as a *viva*) where those with specific expertise in the student's chosen field will be invited to interrogate their knowledge and challenge their findings.

Recording and presenting research under the strictures of academic rigor is often experienced by students as the hardest challenge of their doctoral journey and the point at which they feel most 'at sea'. For the professional doctoral student there is an added challenge to this process, however, as the submitted piece of work is not usually intended as the final destination of the voyage. As Burgess et al. point out, the process of doctoral research may reach its conclusion with the submitted portfolio or thesis but the question then arises about the long-term product of this endeavor:

> There is a continuing tension around the distinction between the process of undertaking a doctorate and the product of this process. If the product of the professional doctorate is to be a means for the development of the profession, how can this occur without full and effective dissemination (assuming again, that this does not fall on stony ground?). There is a long established framework for the growth and evolution of academic knowledge via networks, conferences and journals – is this clear or well developed for the development of 'professional knowledge'? (Burgess, Weller, & Wellington, 2011, p. 15)

NEW WATERS

The cardinal themes we have considered so far embrace a broad spectrum which includes actions, temporality, social relationships, intrapersonal domains of emotional responses, identity and positioning, and organizational structures, systems and demands. Ultimately, however, the professional doctoral voyage will lead to reaching a destination, although whether or not this will be the arrival point which was anticipated at the point of embarkation may be uncertain. Some students may feel that they have arrived in 'new waters' well before their final submission when they begin to recognize change occurring in their professional contexts resulting from the impact of their research. On a personal level, students can also become acutely aware of changes in their identities resulting from their new role as researchers. As Scott and Morrison argue, the impact of becoming a professional doctoral student can be profoundly unsettling:

> Professional doctorates…with their weak boundaries between disciplinary and practicum knowledge, may create different forms of identity in the student. Yet, what is significant (cf. Scott et al., 2004) is that even in professional doctorates the discipline retains a more powerful hold for many students than the profession. During the various rites of passage from competent professional, to novice doctoral initiate, through to finally achieving doctoral status at the convocation ceremony, 'schizophrenic' tendencies are averted for some students by the compartmentalization of identities whilst at university and in professional employment – one being 'academic' and the other 'professional'. (2010, p. 25)

However an alternative view can be posited that rather than maintaining these separate paths of knowledge creation the professional doctorate may, in fact, offer an opportunity to establish a dynamic engagement between the professional ('applied') and academic ('pure') realms of knowledge which have traditionally been regarded as being in tension (Flint & Costley, 2010). They point to the possibility of conceiving this "…as an emerging dialogical approach to learning *for*, *in* and *through* work by means of 'research education'" (Flint & Costley, 2010, p. 12). The exciting potential for the professional doctorate may therefore lie not only with the individual student and their professional contexts but also with society at large. In considering this intersection of the symbiotic domains of practice and research, notions of knowledge mobilization have become dominant within the discourse of some professions, such as medicine and education. The concept of knowledge mobilization bears strong resonance for the professional doctoral researcher who may be uniquely well-positioned to facilitate the multidirectional movement "of both academic and professional knowledge between multiple partners and sites" (Ng-A-Fook et al., 2015) encapsulated in this idea.

CONCLUDING REMARKS

This introductory chapter has sought to highlight the key themes which can be identified as running through each of the chapters that follow and its maritime metaphor provides a unifying vision, attempting to encapsulate the nature and spirit of the professional doctorate programme. As we set out to join the student and staff voyagers it is worth keeping this framework of cardinal themes in mind to help us to navigate through and across these individual journeys so that we can begin to map out the landscape of professional doctoral research and discover what it may offer.

REFERENCES

Bourdieu, P. (1980). *The logic of practice*. Stanford, CA: Stanford University Press.
Bourdieu, P. (1984). *Distinction: A social critique of the judgement of taste*. London: Routledge.
Burgess, H., Weller, G., & Wellington, J. (2011). Tensions in the purpose and impact of professional doctorates. *Work Based Learning e-Journal, 2*(1), 1–20.
Burton, R. L., & Kirshbaum, M. N. (2013). Supporting international students on professional doctorate programmes: A perspective from the United Kingdom. *Work-Based Learning e-Journal International, 3*(1), 109–121.
Costley, C., & Lester, S. (2012). Work-based doctorates: Professional extension at the highest levels. *Studies in Higher Education, 37*(3), 257–269.
Flint, K., & Costley, C. (2010). Critical perspectives on researching the professional doctorate. *Work-Based Learning e-Journal, 1*(1), 1–14.
Flint, K. J., & Barnard, A. (2010, March 29). *The power of development: A critical exploration of a dialogical approach towards student scholarship in higher education*. Annual Learning and Teaching Conference at Nottingham Trent University, Nottingham.
Hughes, C., & Tight, M. (2013). The metaphors we study by: The doctorate as a journey and/or as work. *Higher Education Research and Development, 32*(5), 765–775. doi:10.1080/07294360.2013.777031
Navarro, Z. (2006). In search of cultural interpretation of power. *Institute of Development Studies Bulletin, 37*(6), 11–22.
Ng-A-Fook, N., Butler, J. K., Glithero, L., & Forte, R. (2015). Brokering knowledge mobilization networks: Policy reforms, partnerships, and teacher education. *Education Policy Analysis Archives, 23*(122), 1–28.
Piercy, H., & Gordon, F. (2015). Different but the same: Doctoral students' experiences of multi-professional education. *American Journal of Educational Research, 3*(4), 393–398. doi:10.12691/education-3-4-2
Rudduck, J., & McIntyre, D. (2007). *Improving learning through consulting pupils*. London: Routledge.
Ryan, Y., & Viete, R. (2009). Respectful interactions: Learning with international students in the English-speaking academy. *Teaching in Higher Education, 14*(3), 303–314.
Scott, D., & Morrison, M. (2010). New sites and agents for research education in the United Kingdom: Making and taking doctoral identities. *Work-based Learning e-Journal, 1*(1), 15–34.
Wellington, J. (2013). Searching for 'doctorateness'. *Studies in Higher Education, 38*(10), 1490–1503. doi:10.1080/03075079.2011.634901

PART 1

MAPPING DOCTORAL PRACTICES

PAMELA BURNARD

2. THE PROFESSIONAL DOCTORATE

INTRODUCTION

In the light of significant national and international policy[1] change impacting institutions of higher education and higher education's role in the emerging world economy (Friedman, 2005), it is unsurprising that new interest in the doctoral education field has prompted changing conceptualisations of what doctoral work is. At the level of programme development and provision, universities are increasing the range of practices and number of doctorates on offer. In different countries and in different ways, there are lively ongoing debates about the research doctorate. In a seminal text on the changing practices of doctoral education, Boud and Lee (2009) examine new and emerging forms of doctoral programmes in the UK, Australia and the US, ending with a call to readdress the general neglect of the students' perspective of doing doctoral work. Given the domain of academic practice that was traditionally thought of as most characteristically the purview of universities, the research doctorate in general, and the professional doctorate in particular, is now the focus of public policy and the gaze of governments (Costley & Stephenson, 2009).

The growing numbers of doctorate programmes has seen the emergence of a body of research and inquiry into new and different kinds of doctoral programmes (Boud & Lee, 2009) alongside the traditional doctorate, or PhD (Storey, 2013). The distinction relates to several principles of the professional doctorate researcher at the junction of practice and theory and is a central tenet of their coming to an understanding of their professional workplace or context. These principles can be summarized as identifying the professional doctorate researcher: (a) as a researching professional, and (b) as the research instrument, with significant implications for positioning and critical reflexivity (Lunt, 2002; Fink, 2006).

Current debates and contestations about the range and practices of professional and traditional doctorates are well documented (Scott, Brown, Lunt, & Thorne, 2009; Storey, 2013). Heath's (2006) research with Doctorates of Education suggests that how they are constructed relates to different values placed on knowledge which affect matters such as supervision. Studies have also explored the connection with professional contexts. A generic work-based professional doctorate featured the study of capability including its development and experience by Doncaster and Lester (2002). The importance, interaction and distinctive relationship between the three different settings – the university, the profession and the workplace – centrally

P. Burnard et al. (Eds.), Transformative Doctoral Research Practices for Professionals, 15–28.

involved in the professional doctorate, was examined in a study of the role of environments by Malfroy and Yates (2003). In Australia, Maxwell (2003) explored the emergence of what was coined the 'second generation' of professional doctorates. Several studies in Australia, the UK and the US have compared professional and traditional doctorates (see for example Fink, 2006; Malfroy, 2005; Thorne & Francis, 2001; Boud & Lee, 2009; Streitwieser & Ogden, 2016). The research on professional doctorates (as the term is used in this chapter and across the volume) is understood as providing two insights: firstly, that there is a considerable growth of literature concerning professional doctorates and secondly, that how they are constructed related to different values placed on knowledge and the new knowledge economy.

There are powerful implications for the production and legitimation of *knowledge* within the doctorate worldwide (McWilliam, 2009); in this chapter, as with the book, we are not offering a critique or promoting an essentialist comparison as a kind of shortcut to highlight the dualities of EdD and PhD doctorates. Rather, the central purpose of this chapter, as with the other chapters in this book, and particularly those of Part 1, is to express the range, diversity and fluidity of different perspectives relating to, supporting and redefining the professional doctorate. In doing this, I will argue for a more nuanced view of 'professional doctorate' practices; an interconnected space and journeying between the researcher and the researched that can lead to a dialectical construction of knowledge and a relational stance that becomes transformative for 'researching professionals' (a term which is discussed later).

The increasing internationalization of higher education has also facilitated and encouraged the mobility of doctoral students and, with this, the expansion of traditional (PhD) doctoral programmes. The doctoral education literature is heavily weighted towards the traditional doctorate, in the sense of doctoral education meaning the 'PhD' path. There is a rich and growing field of research on doctoral writing pedagogies: from early work by Connell (1985) to recent studies (Kamler & Thomson, 2014); collections of narratives of PhD doctoral experiences (Lee, Blackmore, & Seal, 2013); and accounts of becoming and being a PhD doctoral student and the implementation and facilitation of doctoral education (Thomson & Walker, 2010). In all cases it is the traditional doctorate that receives most attention. Drawing from US and UK contexts, Storey (2013) illustrates a range of roles and settings that implement innovative approaches to the redesign of professional doctorate programmes and practices that differ "from a typical PhD programme" (p. xv). The rethink involves the adoption of 'Critical Friends' as advisors, facilitators and confidants, who reflect on questions and challenges that emerge during the EdD journeying. A range of EdDs are drawn and charted including online EdD programmes, scholarly practitioner doctoral programmes, EdDs in Educational Leadership and EdDs in principalship. I see this as especially pertinent in rapidly changing times where traditional conceptualisations of doctorates are increasingly being questioned.

With respect to the general notion of 'doctorateness', Denicolo and Park (2013, p. 192) argue that the imperative for a doctorate programme is to update and re-envision the ways in which we conceptualise the doctorate. They make the case for: new market opportunities; new stakeholder (including employer) expectations of what doctorates can potentially offer them as contributors to the generation and use of knowledge; and a workplace culture of innovation and knowledge creation. The key issues concern how "to secure the quality and standards of academic awards and enhance the student experience" (p. 192); and how "'to meet divergent student needs" (p. 196). Questions arise: What does it mean to be a professional doctorate student and educator? Why do professional doctorates work for professionals from different occupational groups?[2] How do professionals come together to form professional doctorate research communities who delight in exploring together synergies between professional practice, specialized knowledge in professions and within the workplace of the profession, academic disciplines and education as a region of knowledge?

As we listen to the views and voices of a particular EdD cohort, examine specific stakeholder viewpoints and see how changes and developments are enacted and choices made by professionals (whose credibility is increasingly acknowledged by the research community), it seems that the Doctor of Education (or EdD) itself is an undocumented mystery that continues to gain recognition.

What characterises the professional doctorate within the changing contexts for doctoral education in universities? What are the demands and challenges that matter the most? What can be said about the relation of the doctoral 'candidate' – a distinctive kind of scholar-practitioner[3] – to their workplace, and to the professional learning communities within their particular workplace, with reference to both professional practice and representation? The term being construed here, 'researching professional', best represents the distinctive relationality and relational dynamic between the full time 'professional' and their relative positioning as researchers 'researching' in their own workplace, who see themselves in a phase of career development that is appropriate for becoming a 'researching professional'. They find themselves encouraged to new aspirational levels. They become aware of how their careers might be changing at a time in the growth of doctoral programmes where there is increasing actual and virtual, mobility – of people, ideas, values and resources.

This chapter develops a case for harnessing the insights from researching professionals who are enrolled on a particular doctorate designed for professionals (see http://www.educ.cam.ac.uk/courses/graduate/doctoral/edd/ where we refer to the term 'researching professionals'). As they critically revisit their practice, assumptions and values, generating an outsider's perspective on their own workplace, we come to recognize how researching professionals engage in educational doctorates, develop identities which become multiple, flexible and changing. Why is that? I argue that, in the context of such change, and as their researcher positioning changes during the course of time, across, and between multiple and discrete phases of research, they develop to become critically reflexive researchers who are asking work-based and work-place questions. They are focused on changing and theorizing professional practices that are facilitated in the context of their own professional workplace.

This is not a chapter which seeks to compare the traditional Doctorate of Philosophy and/or promote the Doctorate of Education. What I do aim to do is to define what is distinctive about the 'professional' doctorate.

The term 'professional doctorate' originated in the US, at Harvard University. This, however, is a chapter in a book which is the product of a UK university where all of those on the EdD are 'researching professionals' (Bourner, Katz, & Watson, 2000; Fink, 2006).

What follows is an introductory discussion of some of the defining features of the researching professional, before Part 2 authors provide context-specific chapters relating each contributor's unique personal story and professional pathway to becoming a researching professiona. It is our hope that this may prompt those in countries where these terms are not current to reflect on whether all doctorates are in fact the same. There are a whole host of similarities, but where there are differences these need to be discussed, problematized and theorized.

THE RESEARCHING PROFESSIONAL

The nature of every profession – every 'job', for that matter – has its own knowledge base: this is partly a function of different forms of knowledge and how professional knowledge develops. The way we view professions is influenced by our experiences, our culture and the traditions within which we live and work. However, it is valuable to challenge our understanding through experiencing other views; different types of knowledges are then brought into dialogue with each other. A crucial point here, and a recurring question in this volume, concerns the role of different kinds of research practices to support the continuous development, self-renewal, and indeed, transformation of professionals. And this process of knowledge creation and training for professionals must be a continuous one, since society continues to change very quickly, constantly making new demands on professional practice. The imperative difference between professional and everyday practice, however, is that the first draws on theoretical knowledge, whereas everyday practice usually does not. Professional practice bridges everyday practice and scientific practice as it combines knowledge from both. What is distinctive about doctorates for professionals is that practice is a central focus and acts as a driver for change. The importance of professional knowledge creation – with its places (often in communities) of professional practice which may be characterized in terms of what lies at the heart of professional doctorates – is the drawing together of what is based upon a recognition of the distinctive contribution of both experiential and scientific knowledge to bring about knowledge creation in 'professional practice'.

All professionals engage in continuous professional learning. In many professions, the membership is expected to review the journals of their field and to attend conferences. They observe each other's practice at work. They often offer feedback that leads to reflective practice. Professionals are characterized by a codified knowledge base, which can be increased consistently through ongoing research – and, as professionals, are expected to maintain familiarity with practitioner research guided by practice or practice informed by research (see Figure 1). Within education this activity remains located primarily in schools and is schools-based research rather than exploring practice in the workplace orientated by knowledge about research, undertaking and using research where the researcher is the instrument of practice.

Often practitioner researchers choose to engage with research, and explore practice which is informed by research in partnership with universities (see, in particular, teacher research and school partnerships, explored by McLaughlin, Black-Hawkins, & McIntyre, 2007). Researching professionals doing EdDs engage in research which is not only guided by their professional practice: the researching professional is the research instrument. Saying the researcher is the research instrument has significant implications for the researcher's roles and responsibilities, positioning and reflexivity. Researchers choose to engage as researching professionals who are increasingly co-constructing new relationships between theory and practice rather than doctorates, which are seen as degrees that exist at the junction of practice and theory.

Here, the underlying argument is that any notion of the 'researching professional' is associated with how they encounter the professional practices and the sustained currency of 'work-based' practices. As MacIntyre (1983, p. 81), cited in Kemmis (2009, p. 22) argues: "Practices must not be confused with institutions. Chess, physics and medicine are practices; chess clubs, laboratories, universities, and hospitals are institutions". I argue that the practice of 'researching professionals' extend beyond practitioner research, where the kinds of research conducted by practicing teachers (and administrators) in a school setting see their dual role as practitioner and researcher, with the research focused and conducted on their own practice. The professional doctorate or EdD for professionals, however, focuses on issues raised by research that is interconnected with professional practice and professional knowledge, working through career questions and the work-place, within the insider-outsider continuum, re-learning in the workplace, where the focus is on practice. From this perspective, some significant questions emerge around continuing changes in working conditions in professional practice at various career stages and phases. What kind of stance enables researching professionals to explore the power relations within the contexts in which they work? What kinds of democratic approaches to research offer guidance and ways of working relationally and also offer improved opportunities for wider participation and influence in decision-making in the broader landscapes in which researching professionals' roles and identities are positioned? How is critical reflexivity applied as a technique which questions the positions, identities and ethicality between the researcher and the researched? How do researching professionals position themselves to address agency and power relationships? How does researcher positioning change across doctoral journeying? These questions and reflexive processes reverberate throughout this book.

Positioning Changes and Critical Reflexivity

In professional doctorate practices the "researcher *is* the instrument". Therefore the task of explicitly putting reflexivity to work and identifying oneself is important. In order to clarify your researcher identity and stance vis-à-vis participants, you must, as Gray (2008, p. 936) notes, "address questions of the researcher's biographical relationship to the topic", such as gender, ethnicity and socioeconomic status, as well as acknowledging the levels of privilege and power conferred by personal history. In professional doctorate research, researching professionals need to challenge their self-understanding and how they interpret the degree of privilege their position carries. Practising critical reflexivity must engage the researching professional's understanding of subjectivity, intersubjectivity, voice, representation and text. With reference to reflexivity specifically, Pillow (2010) advises that 'data' should be analysed responsively and reflexively, and points out that the positioning might change from a postmodern stance to a poststructuralist stance.

The researching professional occupies a privileged place – the insider – with both feet firmly grounded in the cultural systems of their workplace. Yet there may not be such a clear boundary between 'outsider' and 'insider' for the professional researcher, particularly when set in the context of the workplace where there are many 'tribes' at play. It may also be necessary at times to think outside the actual context and reflect as an 'outsider', in order to compare what was seen and heard within the context of another perspective. Would what was being observed in one part of the workplace happen in another? Or, how do different values and meanings relate across different national and socio-historical cultural contexts? Whose meanings? When are understandings shared? Or, how are boundary objects, such as national assessments or national aims in education, or reports and their analysis, made an explicit part of the research and how does the positioning of researchers affect research aims and outcomes? How do researching professionals benefit from understanding and engagement across the boundaries of national cultural values? Thiery (1978) defines bilingualism according to the perceptions of others about social and cultural equivalence. There may not, therefore, be a clear boundary to researcher positioning for professionals. The fluidity between functioning as an insider and an outsider becomes an essential research tool, developing in finesse across the diverse phases and projects of the doctorate, particularly if it is a portfolio designed doctorate.

The various dimensions of the doctoral researcher's background, or role status, in terms of professional and personal attributes, position the researcher in relation to the researched who take part in the study. How the boundaries between these various professional and personal attributes are fixed and interact with each other vary. For example, a professional woman with experience of working in a male-dominated workplace may relate to female experiences of discrimination. The cultural and cross-cultural values of people, places, and institutions matter, and what is important is embedded in the workplace policy priorities, discourse and practices. Thus, being able to position themselves as insiders and outsiders as the situation demands is an important practice for researching professionals. Being an ex-insider researcher with knowledge of the region and workplace context is different to being an insider as a teacher who has already gained trust and has been identified as a teacher colleague, with the "embodied situatedness" (Sultana, 2007) of the insider.

How researchers view *themselves* in the research process, as well as the *identity* of the researching professional, can shift, depending on the situation and the status of the researcher as an insider or outsider responding to the social, political and cultural values of a given context or moment. The EdD is for professionals. The professional doctorate extends over a 5-year period. The portfolio research plan can progress over 3 years in one community or workplace. The insiderness and outsiderness can be seen as a balancing act between the positioning that the researching professional actively takes and the ways in which their role is defined by how others involved in the project, either as participants or those further afield, view the researcher. The image researchers have of themselves, and how others in the community view them, highlights the importance of power and privilege: it influences how participants view a researcher who is researching from inside the community. The shifting positioning may be reflective of a conscious effort in research design not to remain an insider or outsider. The participants may be in awe of an outsider with whom building meaningful relationships takes time and which may also be difficult. The participative methods used may contribute to the researching professional changing position within the workplace. Shifting such positioning and building relationships of trust means the development of an 'inbetweener' researcher stance which challenges traditional dichotomies of the insider and outsider.

Researching One's Own Profession in One's Own Workplace: A Privileged Place

There is recognition of power biases, which need to be addressed in any research, not only in terms of whom the gatekeepers of knowledge are but also in terms of how 'objective' facts and 'subjective' truths are addressed. For researching professionals the research interview creates a platform for knowledge exchange and emotional meetings; sometimes disclosure of the person being interviewed; and, sometimes, a therapeutic tool for telling the story of experiences that are not often told, understood or appreciated. Otherwise uneven power relations, can, to some degree, even out. This allows for some collaboration and knowledge co-construction. Depending on the identity of the researcher – whether as an outsider, a woman, an adult, a teacher-figure, or a combination of all of these identities; or a conspirator, a colleague, a knowledgeable expert, a coach, a mentor or a friend – some participants may omit important information about themselves, even when prompted.

The use of participative techniques can assist in how researcher positioning changes. Researchers can contribute to a shift in how participants see them – for instance, to where they are viewed as someone who has a genuine interest in the lives and opinions of the participants. Thomson and Gunter (2010) have argued against the fixed and dichotomous notions of 'insiderness' and 'outsiderness'. However, the active term of 'inbetweener' also recognizes that the researcher can be proactive in their attempts to place themselves in between.

Power Relations

Through the lens of Pierre Bourdieu's theories and tools we can visualise how power operates between different groups in society and shed light on how it might affect data collection in a research interview context as well as the professional context. Bourdieu (1979) describes an individual's assets and resources as capital. The acquisition and mastery of different forms of capital can guarantee a diversity of power holdings depending on the type of capital, and the field in which they operate. Groups, classes and families develop strategies to maintain or increase capital holdings or discourage others from doing so. In a society, different groups have different cultural capital depending on where you come from and what groups you belong to. For groups with an immigrant background, the interpretation of cultural capital and class identification and status can sometimes become complicated (Burnard, Hofvander Trulsson, & Söderman, 2015).

Social mobility, downward mobility, social immobility or class remobility are all examples of how different capitals can play out in research contexts. Researching families with immigrant background, living in exile, we have noticed among them a recurrent will to verbally position themselves, in regard to class background (economic and cultural), reasons for their situation in the new country and their aspirations (Hofvander Trulsson & Burnard, 2015). These perspectives of positioning in the interview setting, where gender, class and cultural imprints impact the way people talk and present themselves, are central to the use of reflexive analysis strategies in professional doctorate research. Pillow (2010) invites us to interrupt these common practices and engage with new culturally reflexive and ethical tools for researcher reflexivity: for collecting data, equalising the research relationships, doing data collection 'with' instead of 'on', and for practices that lead to 'multi-vocal' texts and the exploration of differing writing and representation styles.

The idea of the professional who bridges both research and practice is what we are using to describe the 'researching professional'. There is a growing class of hybrid 'scholar-practitioners', more often referred to as 'teacher-researchers' or 'researcher-practitioners' who often work as senior managers or, in school sectors as head teachers. These are people who bridge research and practice: that is, they both 'study it' and 'do it'. Streitwieser and Ogden 2016, p. 27) have helped practitioners take a new view of professional action and advocate research into the kind of thinking that underlies and helps explain the way professionals carry out their work. The professional knowing that derives from professionals completing doctorates (such as EdDs) within their workplace, and use of their field's terminology to appropriately converse with key stakeholders, leveraging that understanding to reflect critically and reflexively on their daily practice with authority and disseminate their thinking and publish during the course of the doctorate, is growing.

With recent growth in higher education enrolments, there are now many new doctoral paths that go beyond the traditional doctorate (PhD). While many come to do a PhD, many come to international education positions with specialized education and professional training and seek advancement through promotion and reassignment, from related professions or the faculty ranks, looking for career routes through professional degrees, such as the MBA (Streitwieser & Oden, 2016, p. 25). Professionals seeking to do doctorates can be those who are outside observers of higher education, interested in higher-level research training, who are less interested in becoming academics who go on to doctoral work within universities. They can be academics interested in professional practice or key leaders from influential professional associations and private organisations. They can also be educators and practitioners who manage the daily logistical flow of students and personnel or academics/scholars who conduct research, collect and analyze data, and publish findings to inform, improve and justify the activity, but who are looking to consider how scholarship and practice could function in grater harmony.

In Figure 1, the 'scholar-practitione' is represented with particular reference to research guided by practice and practice informed by research. Figure 2 illustrates the distinctiveness of the 'researching professional' and professional doctorate with its relationship between research embedded (rather than guided) practice and practice embedded in research.

Streitwieser and Ogden (2016) argue the distinctiveness between practitioners 'who do it' and scholars 'who study it' as simplistic and false, neither necessarily precluding nor prioritizing the other' (p. 13). Yet, often, the context of researching professional practice in the workplace for the researching professional is not a clear dichotomy separating research and practice but rather one where their research both guides their practice and informs their practice simultaneously.

Closely allied to professional doctorates, especially those which require the researching professional to establish professional learning communities, are Wenger's (1998) ideas concerning the construction of *communities of practice*, particularly his definition of communities of practice as "groups of people who share a concern or a passion for something they do and learn how to do it better as they interact regularly" (1998, p. 1). Wenger's codification of the three characteristics of a community of practice (i.e. a shared domain of "mutual interest" where the community "engages reciprocally" as members who interact and learn together and the practice of a group of practitioners in which members "develop a shared repertoire of resources: experiences, stories, tools, ways of addressing recurring problems") are constructed

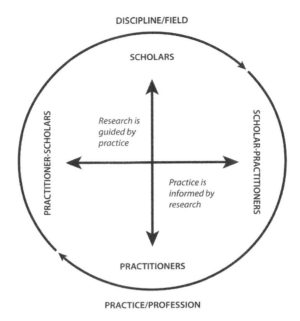

Figure 1. The scholar-practitioner and practitioner-scholar differentiated

and explored between three different environments – the university, the profession and the workplace – where what is relevant to educational theory, policy and practice informs the context which is specific to the researching professional.

The confluence of the critical, interrelated factors that are the defining features of the professional doctorate (as shown in Figure 2) indicates how 'policy' is the background upon which the 'practice', 'theory' and 'knowledge' operate. The direction of influence for policy often tends to be one-directional: that is, rarely are government policies influenced by practice, theory and knowledge. Policy operates upon those circles of theory/practice/knowledge, often in ways that facilitate and shape them (at best), or limit and constrain them, or (at worst) undermine them. From studies of professional doctorates, we can see how effective use of research and scholarship play a significant role in shaping the direction of the field and profession over time. Similarly, practice and theory can inform the direction and advancement of the profession and the field (Streitwieser & Ogden, 2016). With the insistence and strong global focus of the *new knowledge economy,* and discourses in the university, the workplace and the professions, there is a growing emphasis on the external drivers for the growth of professional doctorates and knowledge creation in and across professional learning communities, as well as on the professional training and continuing professional development of practitioners; their involvement in

Figure 2. The professional doctorate – its purpose and distinctiveness

knowledge production also gives rise to a changing conception of knowledge. We see this in the chapters that follow in Part 2.

CLOSING REFLECTIONS

Professional doctorates have emerged in a wide range of academic disciplines with the Doctorate of Education having the largest market in the UK (UKCGE, 2002). The drivers for the development of professional doctorates, as argued earlier in this chapter, are: the internationalization of higher education; the globablized knowledge market; the new knowledge economy; and an increasing need for a critical approach by professionals and professional learning communities to their knowledge-base and functions. As part of this changing picture, professional doctorates have grown rapidly in the UK, Australia and the US. A richer knowledge, termed 'creative knowledge', is generated within and on the boundaries between academia and the creative economy. The concepts of knowledge transfer (often labelled knowledge exchange or external engagement), and 'creative human capital' (developed within professional learning communities), create opportunities for shared research and innovation. This has become increasingly important in the relationship between HE and knowledge creation within academia and the work and practice of professionals. The value of shared research and innovation have been framed explicitly in relation to educational partnerships, collaborations across HE institutions and school sectors, and collaboration with small and medium size organisations within the creative and cultural industries (Bennett & Burnard, 2016).

The authors in this book generally, and in those in Part 1 specifically, explore the meaning of the professional doctorates. They are aware that, in addressing what we understand, as a result of the internationalisation of higher education, as the professional doctorate may not be the same in the United States as it is in the United Kingdom or elsewhere in the world. In many aspects there will indeed be differences. In other parts of the world, the practitioners who do scholarly work within their professional learning and academic communities are referred to as scholar-practitioners or practitioner-scholars, or practitioner researchers. The chapters in this part of the volume bring their own perspectives on the role of the researching professional to the idea of the professional whose research explores the issue of the interaction and relationship between the three different environments – the workplace, the profession and the university – and has a significant impact on practice, theory, policy and knowledge. Each contributor shares their own unique personal story and professional pathway to becoming a researching professional.

We want to offer a different way of thinking about the work of doctoral education and doctoral research for professionals and their professional learning communities. We want to invite colleagues who are working in doctoral education, who are forming identities as researching professionals with a focus on professional practice, and/or deciding to embark on a professional doctorate, to think about how we understand the multifaceted practice of doctorates in education in general and the professional doctorate in particular, and what each individual university doctoral educator thinks it is.

We invite you to explore the implicit theories individual lecturers and supervisors have about the Doctorate of Education, its purposes and implications for its critical aspects of pedagogy. Other issues that give rise to forward thinking about the distinctiveness of professional doctorates are concerned with how views are shared, how staff is inducted into the teaching teams and the interface between the professional work-based learning community and the university. What further developments, in ways of thinking about what it means to be a professional doctorate student and educator, can result in new perspectives, voices, journeyings and pedagogic practices in professional doctorates?

In the spirit of this chapter, our Part 1 focuses with Karen Ottewell and Wai Mun Lim ((both of whom have PhDs and are embarking on a (second) professional (work-based) doctorate)) on the connection between professional context and professional doctorate practices and with Simon Dowling on imperatives for those embarking on funded professional (work-based) doctorates; and in the volume as a whole, we invite you to continue the conversation with us, your peers, your doctoral students, and your researching professional colleagues.

NOTES

1. For the latest policy reforms which are about transforming Higher Education in UK see Higher Education White Paper https://www.gov.uk/government/publications/higher-education-success-as-a-knowledge-economy-white-paper and Green Paper http://blog.universitiesuk.ac.uk/2015/11/06/a-summary-of-the-higher-education-green-paper/ For a Singaporean EdD See http://www.nie.edu.sg/higher-degrees/doctor-in-education-edd

2. Occupational groups represented on the 5-year EdD programme at the Faculty of Education include physiotherapy, counselling, engineering, veterinary science, artist, service, organisational and company management, administration, school leaders, head teachers, senior managers, consultants, life coaches, health workers, computer scientists, subject specialist teachers, inspectors, school and college governors, biochemistry, architecture and design, senior executives, teacher educators.

3. The category of researching professional, who spans both research and practice, is referred to as 'scholar-practitioners', a term coined by Bernhard Streitwieser and Anthony Ogden (2016) in a book entitled 'International Higher Education's Scholar-Practitioners'. They argue the distinction between practitioners 'who do it' (that is, scholarly work) and scholars 'who 'study it' is reductive, 'simplistic and false, neither necessarily precluding nor prioritizing the other' (p. 13).

REFERENCES

Bennett, D., & Burnard, P. (2016). Human capital career creativities. In R. Comunian & A. Gilmore (Eds.), *Higher education and the creative economy: Beyond the campus* (pp. 123–142). London: Routledge.

Boud, D., & Lee, A. (Eds.). (2009). *Changing practices of doctoral education*. London: Routledge.

Bourdieu, P. (1979). *Outline of a theory of practice*. Cambridge: Cambridge University Press.

Bourdieu, P. (1984). *Distinction: A social critique of the judgement of taste*. London: Routledge.

Bourner, T., Katz, T., & Watson, D. (Eds.). (2000). Professional doctorates: The development of researching professionals. In T. Bourner, T. Katz, & D. Watson (Eds.), *New directions in professional higher education*. SRHE Buckingham: Open University Press

Burnard, P., Hofvander Trulsson, Y., & Soderman, J. (2016). *Bourdieu and the sociology of music education*. London: Routledge.

Connell, R. W. (1985). How to supervise a PhD. *Vestes, 2*, 38. Retrieved January 5, 2008, from www.ph.uimelb.edu/au/pgss/2520/node33.html

Costley, C., & Stephenson, J. (2009). *Building doctorates around individual candidates' professional experience* (pp. 171–186). London: Routledge.

Denicolo, P., & Park, C. (2013). Doctorateness – An elusive concept? In M. Kompf & P. Denicolo (Eds.), *Critical issues in higher education* (pp. 191–199). The Netherlands: Sense Publishers.

Doncaster, K., & Lester, S. (2002). Capability and its development experience from a work-based doctorate. *Studies in Higher Education, 27*(1), 91–100.

Fink, D. (2006). The professional doctorate: Its relativity to the PhD and relevance for the knowledge economy. *International Journal of Doctoral Studies, 1*(1), 35–44.

Friedman, T. L. (2005). *The world is flat. A brief history of the twenty-first century*. New York, NY: Furrar, Straus and Giroux.

Gray, B. (2008). Putting emotion and reflexivity to work in researching migration. *Sociology, 42*(5), 935–952.

Heath, H. (2006). Supervision of professional doctorates: Education doctorates in English universities. *Higher Education Review, 38*(2), 21–39.

Hofvander Trulsson, Y., & Burnard, P. (2016). Insider, outsider or cultures in-between: Ethical and methodological considerations in intercultural arts research. In P. Burnard, E. Mackinlay, & K. Powell (Eds.), *The Routledge international handbook of intercultural arts research* (pp. 115–125). London: Routledge.

Kamler, B., & Thomson, P. (2014). *Helping doctoral students write: Pedagogies for supervision.* London: Routledge.

Kemmis, S. (2009). Understanding professional practice: A synoptic framework. In B. Green (Ed.), *Understanding and researching professional practice* (pp. 19–38). Rotterdam, The Netherlands: Sense Publishers.

Kompf, M., & Denicolo, P. (Eds.). (2013). *Critical issues in higher education.* The Netherlands: Sense Publishers.

Lee, E., Blackmore, C., & Seal, E. (2013). *Research journeys: A collection of narratives of the doctoral experience.* Newcastle upon Tyne: Cambridge Scholars Publishing.

Lunt, I. (2002). *Professional doctorates.* London: UKCGE.

Malfroy, J. (2005). Doctoral supervision, workplace research and changing pedagogic practices. *Higher Education Research and Development, 24*(2), 165–178.

Malfroy, J., & Yates, L. (2003) Knowledge in action: Doctoral programmes forging new identities. *Journal of Higher Education Policy and Management, 25*(2), 119–129.

McLaughlin, C., Black-Hawkins, K., & McIntyre, D. (2007). *Networking practitioner research.* London: Routledge.

McWilliam, E. (2009). Doctoral education in risky times. In D. Boud & A. Lee (Eds.), *Changing practices in doctoral education* (pp. 189–199). London: Routledge.

Merton, R. (1972). Insiders and outsiders: A chapter in the sociology of knowledge. *American Journal of Sociology, 78*, 9–47.

Pillow, W. S. (2010). Dangerous reflexivity: Rigour, responsibility and reflexivity in qualitative research. In P. Thomson & M. Walker (Eds.), *The Routledge doctoral student's companion: Getting to grips with research in education and the social sciences* (pp. 270–282). London: Routledge.

Scott, D., Brown, A., Lunt, I., & Thorne, L. (2009). *Specialised knowledge in UK professions: Relations between state, the university and the workplace* (pp. 143–156). London: Routledge.

Storey, V. (Ed.). (2013). *Redesigning professional education doctorates.* New York, NY: Palgrave MacMillan.

Streitwieser, B., & Ogden, A. C. (Eds.). (2016). *International higher education's scholar-practitioners: Bridging research and practice.* Oxford, UK: Symposium Books.

Sultana, F. (2007). Reflexivity, positionality and participatory ethics: Negotiating fieldwork dilemmas in international research. *ACME: An International Journal for Critical Geographies, 6*(3), 374–385.

Thiery, C. (1978). True bilingualism and second-language learning. In D. Gerver & H. Sinaiko (Eds.), *Interpretation and communication* (pp. 145–153). New York, NY: Plenum Press.

Thomson, P., & Gunter, H. (2010). Inside, outside, upside down: The fluidity of academic researcher 'identity' in working with/in school. *International Journal of Research and Method in Education, 34*(1), 17–30.

Thomson, P., & Walker, M. (Eds.). (2010). *The Routledge doctoral student's companion: Getting to grips with research in education and the social sciences.* London: Routledge.

Thorne, I., & Francis, J. (2001). PhD and professional doctorate experience: The problematics of the National Qualifications Framework. *Higher Education Review, 33*(3), 13–29.

UKCGE. (2002). *Report on professional doctorates.* Dudley: UKCGE.

Wenger, E. (1998). *Communities of practice.* Cambridge, UK: Cambridge University Press.

KAREN OTTEWELL AND WAI MUN LIM

3. PHD: BEEN THERE, DONE THAT

So, Why Do a (Second), Professional Doctorate?

INTRODUCTION

You would be forgiven for thinking that doing one doctorate would be enough for anyone. The pure joy (and, admittedly, relief) you feel at having successfully defended what felt like your life's work does make you forget, though, the three years of pain: physical, emotional as well as intellectual. Yet, whilst many may feel at the end of the arduous process of making "a significant contribution to scholarship"[1] that a second doctorate ought to be easier, since you have already *been there and done that*, few actually put this to the test. And why should they? After all, a doctorate is the highest degree awarded by a university – so why would you need two? Yet this is precisely the journey the two authors have chosen to embark upon. Both are university academics, managers and administrators with PhDs, a Doctorate of Philosophy, who have decided to become "researching professionals" (Bourner, Katz, & Watson, 2000) by starting an EdD, a Doctorate of Education. 'But why?' you could be excused for asking. The answer to this lies epistemologically in the different ways in which knowledge is produced and methodologically by the potential impact practitioner knowledge may have: a ripple or a splash? But first, before we share our own critical reflections on the titular question, we need to briefly explore what doctoral study, in all its forms, is and means.

The Five 'Ws' of the Doctorate[2]

The term 'doctorate' derives from the Latin *docere*, which means 'to teach', and it was in this sense of the word that it was originally used in medieval Europe as a licence to teach at a university – *licentia docendi*. However, its usage and meaning have changed over the years; today it is the highest level of degree that a student can achieve, usually requiring, in the UK, three to four years of study, and for which you must conduct 'original' and 'significant' research in a particular field or subject. Yet, whilst the Doctor of Philosophy – better known in its acronym of PhD – is the most common type of doctorate, it is not the only one.

The first doctoral degree was granted in Paris at the end of the twelfth century (Noble, 1994) (and yet it was not until the early nineteenth century that the PhD acquired its modern meaning). For the next 600 years, doctoral programmes in

P. Burnard et al. (Eds.), Transformative Doctoral Research Practices for Professionals, 29–41.

the fields of theology, medicine and law were used as preparation for professional practice (Bourner, Bowden, & Laing, 2001). Early doctorates were, therefore, in essence, what are now commonly referred to as 'professional doctorates', namely "research degrees for practitioners which combine higher learning with research in the workplace" (Taylor, 2007, p. 154), albeit in the sense of *preparing for* compared to *reflecting on* practice from *within the profession*. The Humboldt University in Berlin was the first to award the PhD in the nineteenth century. In the US, Yale was the first in 1861, and the first PhD in the UK, or DPhil as it is known at the UK's oldest university, was at Oxford in 1920. The following year, the first professional doctorate, a Doctor of Education (EdD), was awarded at Harvard.

Whilst the PhD is still the most common type of doctorate, there are now five forms of doctoral degree in the UK (Scott et al., 2004):

1. PhD
2. Practice-based
3. Professional doctorate
4. New Route PhD
5. PhD by portfolio

Although little known outside English-speaking countries (Lunt, 2006), it is the professional doctorate which is on the increase, particularly in Australia, the UK, and the US (Bourner, Bowden, & Laing, 2001). This increase is not coincidental, since higher education has been "asked to adapt to new societal needs, to be more responsive to the world around it"; in short, to consider the "economic applications of knowledge" (Kwiek, 2003, p. 81). Many countries, therefore, now have research policy agendas that suggest and advocate for the advancement of the field of knowledge production in the social sciences broadly, and educational research specifically, to ensure that "products of research can best influence and benefit the development of policy and practice for all parts of society" Gu, 2010, p. 337).

Irrespective of the route of doctoral study, according to the doctoral qualification descriptors outlined in the Framework for Higher Education Qualifications in England, Wales, and Northern Ireland (QAA, 2008), the broad expectations of all forms of doctorate are the same: namely, the creation and interpretation, construction and/or exposition of knowledge which extends the forefront of a discipline, usually through original research. However, as Thomson and Walker (2010b) rightly argue, the test of a doctorate does not rest simply on whether it produces new knowledge, and doctoral work is not simply about acquiring a set of tools and techniques. But whilst "the traditional PhD concept of doctoral enterprise as the production of 'independent, autonomous scholars' as opposed to the 'improved practitioner' still continues" (Taylor, 2007, p. 155), the new "knowledge economy" (McWilliam & James, 2002) is invoking a shift in what constitutes doctoral knowledge.

Whilst the 'what', 'when' and 'where' of the doctorate are rather straightforward to answer, since it has remained globally, in all its developing forms, the highest academic qualification conferred by a university since its inauguration in the twelfth century, the following section will focus in greater detail on the *who* and the *why*, which have both seen distinct shifts.

Differences between a Traditional Doctorate and a Professional Doctorate

This shift in knowledge production can be most clearly seen in the emergence of the new routes in doctoral education outlined above. These developments, supported by the UK Council for Graduate Education, are to be encouraged, since they extend the capacity to change and generate research opportunities from different perspectives as well as contributing to greater student diversity. Within this context, professional doctorates, and amongst these the Doctorate of Education (EdD), have seen the greatest growth over the last decade due to a number of factors, including: an increase in growth of the professional fields; the nature of professional work becoming increasingly complex; and government priorities for improving the professions (Taylor, 2007, p. 154). Universities have therefore diversified in response to the needs of the knowledge economy.

There have been several studies that have explored professional doctorates in relation to the traditional PhD,[3] with some arguing that the two are in essence the same, whilst others argue the contrary. Whilst these arguments tend to share common ground, two contributions to this debate are particularly worth highlighting within the context of the present discussion, since they pinpoint two key distinctions: namely, the *what* and the *who*. In their 2001 article, Bourner, Bowden and Laing cited 20 differences between the two doctoral routes, one of which concerned the starting point for the research, where they noted: "[w]hereas the PhD candidate starts from what is known (that is, the literature review), professional doctorate candidates start from what is *not* known (that is, some perceived problem in professional practice)" (p.72). And whilst it is true that both routes aim at the development of new knowledge, it could be argued, as Taylor (2007) does, that the PhD is aimed at those who wish to become 'professional researchers', whilst the professional doctorate is aimed at those who wish to become 'researching professionals' (Bourner, Katz, & Watson, 2000). These two distinctions may be seen to at least partially outline the reasons why one may choose one route over another, yet the defining differentiation between them, we feel, lies arguably more in their respective epistemological perspectives.

Since the ultimate aim of all forms of doctoral study is to create new knowledge, how one might differentiate between them could be said to hinge on how the different doctorates produce this knowledge. Gibbons et al. provide a useful insight into this in their 1994 work, *The New Production of Knowledge*, in which they proposed a dual mode of knowledge production:

1. *Disciplinary* – which is knowledge constructed in the university; and
2. *Trans-disciplinary* – which is generated through practice and experience.

Mode 2 was seen to be complementary to, rather than a replacement for, Mode 1. The disadvantage of Mode 2 knowledge, however, is that it tends to be local and hence not generalisable. So, bridging this gap, Scott (1995) proposed two further modes:

3. *Dispositional* – encompassing deliberation and reflection, designed to integrate professional and academic knowledge; and
4. *Reflexivity* – explicitly or implicitly designed to change practice through the development of the individual through critical reflection.

Usher (2002) considers Mode 2 knowledge to be the prime objective of the professional doctorate on account of its context of application. By drawing on more than one discipline, it has been suggested that the trans-disciplinary approach can lead to new perspectives that transcend each stand-alone discipline (Choi & Pak, 2006). However, the importance of reflection to developing professional practice has been well documented (Baird et al., 1991) hence it is arguably Scott's (1995) refined introduction of critical reflexivity that is the defining difference. As Maxwell and Shanahan (1997) have noted, professional doctorates must raise epistemological questions about the nature and creation of knowledge, the positioning of knowledge and the relations between those who create it, since these signal a move from the classic model, in which academic groups or individuals determine what type of knowledge is valid. This integration of academic and professional knowledge is central to the professional doctorate, since it is seeking to produce "situated theory entering into and emerging from practice" (Usher, 2002, p. 127). Therefore, what is critical to the production of such situated theory is reflexivity – the awareness of the theorist, here the researching professional, of their unique role in the construction of new knowledge.

Critical reflection and reflexivity are keys to the professional doctorate on account of their relationship with professional practice, where the researcher is the professional practising research within their professional context. This could apply to part-time PhD students, but the distinction with professional doctorates here is to be aware of limitations in our knowledge reflexively: to consider how our own behaviour affects the practices in the organisation we are working for (and examining), and to understand how organisational realities' shared practices are shaped (Bolton, 2005, p. 13).

Critical reflection has been described by Wilson (2002) as a method of scrutinizing our own subjective thoughts about our identities and beliefs. Dewey, on the other hand, suggested that critical reflection is a recurring process of reasoning based on "a conscious and voluntary effort to establish belief upon a firm basis of evidence and rationality" (1993, p. 9). Moreover, since the development of professional practice lies at the heart of professional doctorates, Schön (1983) purports that expertise can only be attained by applying theory to practice via the process of reflection. As researching professionals, this notion of critical reflexivity is central to developing more effective and innovative professional practice.

This dual role of practitioner *and* researcher, which has been deftly referred to by Drake and Heath (2011, p. 25) as "inhabiting the hyphens", basically involves looking into the fishbowl from the outside as an insider, where the positioning of the researcher is uniquely separate from their paid role as a practitioner. This positioning where "one's own presence and perspective influence knowledge and actions" (Fook, 2002, p. 43) is both the defining strength of the professional doctorate whilst at the same time considered by some to be its Achilles' heel. The crux of the objection is that, because the researching professional is more often centrally placed 'in' the field of research, it is difficult, if not impossible, to achieve an appropriate degree of critical distance. As Hajer (1995, p. 53) has noted, "the idea of the role assumes that a person is always separable from that role taken up", but in *inhabiting the hyphens* this is impossible: Practitioner-researchers are simultaneously part of the practice setting *and* the academy, and therefore need to negotiate the practices of the academy as part of their reflexive project, but within the context of professional practice. The subsequent focus on reflexive and critical analysis of practice in a professional capacity and the proposed implementation of change is therefore central to the complex issue of coming to terms with a reflexive professional practice through the research lens, and so is fundamental to the professional doctorate. This also forms perhaps the distinction from the PhD.

From this perspective, the contribution to knowledge in a professional doctorate is not unlike that which Aristotle termed *phronesis*, which roughly translates as a 'practical wisdom' – a new way of knowing which goes beyond *epitome* (knowledge) and *techne* (knowledge in an applied way as in a craft). Having completed a doctorate, we understand *epitome*; as practising academics we possess *techne*. Being candidates of the EdD, we are aspiring towards *phronesis*.

RESEARCHING PROFESSIONAL IN PRACTICE: TWO NARRATIVES

The objective of the following sections is to provide a critically reflective account in which we position the motivations and journeys which brought us to the professional doctorate, whilst also reflecting on how these may be different or indeed similar to our experiences of the PhD. What sets us apart from (arguably) many who choose this route is that, not only have we experienced the process of 'doctoring' (Tennant, 2004), to the extent that we are already 'doctored', but we are also senior academics working in UK higher education. We therefore do not straddle the experiential divide that Taylor (2007, p. 157) highlighted: that of being, on the one hand, more expert than our supervisors in some aspects of professional knowledge, yet, on the other, novices in research and higher level study. Our position is consequently different to that of many who choose this path since, not only have we already been awarded the highest academic degree by that very community whose practices we are now looking to challenge, but since we also both work at universities, the community of practice which we are looking to investigate through the professional doctorate is also the one which is accrediting the EdD. We hope, however, that this will provide a level of insight and reflexivity that is currently lacking in the literature comparing these two doctoral routes.

Narrative 1: Dr Karen Ottewell

Background. To quote Thomson and Walker (2010a, p. 13), my route to the PhD was almost that of "[t]he typical honours graduate proceeding directly to doctoral study" – the only slight difference being that I studied for a Master's degree in between, so, overall, spending an unbroken 22 years in full-time education. My motivation to do the PhD was not because I wanted to become an academic, but was simply out of sheer intellectual curiosity for eighteenth-century German literature, a curiosity that my undergraduate study had kindled but not fulfilled. Being allowed to dedicate three years of my life to researching my chosen specialism was therefore personally rewarding. I can actually remember, however, about six weeks into the PhD, in the University Library, when I realised that the book I was looking for was the one I was writing. This felt like a monumental task. Unlike undergraduate study where, at the end, you are basically assessed on the accumulation of knowledge you have acquired, postgraduate study is different – you are at the top of Bloom's Taxonomy of Learning Domains and are expected to 'create' knowledge (Bloom et al., 1956).

That said, it was a thoroughly character-building experience, not only in being able at the end of the process to be accredited with having made a "significant contribution to scholarship", both by the University and subsequently by the academy after publication, but also as an individual, since a PhD is a phenomenal mental challenge. The experience gave me a resilience that has since been of great benefit both professionally and personally. Amusingly, though, at the time, I quipped that a second doctorate would be much easier to do because I had *been there and done that*. With the much more conscious decision to do a professional doctorate, I am now putting that to the test.

So, why a professional doctorate? The French philosopher Lyotard (1979) argues that knowledge is legitimated by its performativity or capacity to enhance the efficiency and effectiveness of the socio-economic system, which basically encapsulates my motivation to do the professional doctorate. Whilst my PhD may have made an "original and well-researched [...] valuable contribution to eighteenth-century scholarship" (Baughan, 2004, p. 828), with the EdD, I want to make a significant practical impact by enhancing the efficiency and effectiveness of my professional role.

As Director of Academic Development and Training for International Students at the University of Cambridge, my role and that of my team is to support, predominantly, postgraduate students whose first language is not English, in meeting the demands of their research with respect to the development of their academic literacy. I have become, however, increasingly critical of both national and international practices with regard to preparing international students for study and supporting them during their studies at English-speaking universities. The main ground for my critical stance is the fact that much English for Academic Purposes (EAP) provision shows little awareness or understanding of the highly complicated set of processes that are involved in the key skill required of all students at tertiary level, namely academic writing.

Therefore, my primary motivation to do a professional doctorate is simply that this will provide me with a framework of critical reflexivity through which I will be able to research my own and my community's professional practice with a view to being better at my job. I will achieve this not only by being forced to objectively and critically reflect on the nature of international student support but also because, by undergoing this doctoral process again, I will be better placed to understand the process that the students I support are undergoing and will be better able to support them in their development of discipline-specific written academic literacy.

Experience so far? By far the greatest challenge I have experienced has been in coming to terms with doing the professional doctorate both *in* and *at* my own institution. In this I do not simply mean the ethical considerations that researching your own professional context engenders, but far more the different 'roles' (cf. Hajer: 1995) or 'identities' that I now inhabit and must align. To contextualise: I am a University Senior Lecturer and a Graduate Student at the same time in the same institution, where my practitioner role is to support the development of written academic literacy – the very practices of which, however, I am both researching and in the process of (re-) developing myself. I am therefore not only looking into the fishbowl from the outside as an insider, but in the role of researcher I need to practise those very skills that I am researching and which I, as a practitioner, teach.

This refraction of roles and identities is something from which I am going to be able to draw a unique insight, albeit subjective-objectively. To clearly delineate between these various refractions will be challenging, especially since they all overlap, arguably to a greater extent in my case than for the majority of those doing professional doctorates.

Taking a step back from my personal position, though, all academics who teach are basically researching practitioners, albeit in a different sense to what is expected within a professional doctorate. We are continually looking to expand our knowledge of our field and this, in turn, will be carried over into *what* we teach and presumably (hopefully?) *how* we teach. The focus is, of course, different, since the primary driver for academics is to increase their knowledge and understand their subject – Mode One knowledge production (Gibbons et al., 1994). The professional doctorate, however, forces you to reflect not only on the content but on yourself as the practitioner and your community of practice. Given the focus of my professional doctorate, I could have easily carried out this research through a second traditional doctorate – and I was in fact asked this very question in my interview for the EdD programme. But I do not simply wish to theorise on the nature of written academic literacy development by merely designing a new paradigm; as a practitioner I am equally, if not more, interested in the practical application and success of this paradigm. In short, I wish to generate practical impact.

Narrative 2: Dr Wai Mun Lim

Background. I majored in Economics and Sociology as an undergraduate. Unbeknown to me then, these subjects laid the foundation of my epistemological journey. The first years of my post-graduate working life saw the Internet take off and enter a frenzied phase of growth. This led to a desire to acquire management techniques, which would help me to deal with the challenges commonly found in a fast-moving business environment. A very stimulating Masters in Business Administration ensued; I found the dissertation/research project so enriching, I explored the possibility of pursuing an academic career by securing a position as a part-time lecturer. I spent what remained of my time on a part-time PhD investigating the adoption and management of Internet technologies. Like others pursuing a PhD at that time, I viewed the PhD as a necessary induction to the world of academia and research (Brennan, 1995).

As I had left the industry to pursue the PhD, I became an 'outsider' reflecting on my time as a practitioner, while learning new and unfamiliar research skills and getting to grips with theoretical concepts. After obtaining the PhD, I began my career as a lecturer in service management. Fast-forward 8 years: I am now a Senior Lecturer juggling teaching and research with management responsibilities. These activities have culminated in a quest to improve my pedagogical knowledge in order to inform my professional practice in a structured manner. Thus began my EdD journey. In the narrative that follows I provide an account of the various stages of thought and action leading to a fulfilling and buoyant start to my second term on the EdD.

Discovering the issues and 'why a professional doctorate'? My proposed area of research for the professional doctorate evolved over 15 years as an academic practitioner in post-'92 higher education institutions (HEIs); the experience shaped my aspiration to better understand the dynamics of the education sector, in particular the student recruitment and student experience aspects of direct entry degree programmes.

Since my initial foray into academia, efforts have been made to increase Higher Education participation in the UK (Corney, 2003). A sub-degree level qualification known as the Foundation Degree was introduced subsuming other similar qualifications like the Higher National Certificate (HNC) and Higher National Diploma (HND) (Canter, 2006). Students who successfully complete these sub-degree level qualifications are given the opportunity to obtain advance standing in a relevant university degree programme. Before long, overseas educational institutions offering similar 'sub-degree qualifications' were seeking to offer their students a pathway into a UK university with advanced standing. As such inquiries grew, opportunities to contribute to my institution's international recruitment drive grew in tandem, in part because I am a product of an education system in the Far East and am cognisant with the region's cultural and educational contexts.

Meanwhile, the number of students enrolling directly into Level 6 (FHEQ) of various degree programmes appears to be growing. The majority of these students are international, and often face multiple adjustment issues such as proficiency in English language, culture, academic skills and educational background (Andrade, 2006). Not only do the direct entry students have to deal with these adjustment issues, but they are also expected to adapt to the university's administration and teaching approaches while attempting to complete a Bachelor's degree in a year.

Most past studies of international students and trans-national partnerships or agreements in higher education typically focus on definitions (Qiang, 2003), the motivation for internationalising (Altbach & Knight, 2007), the teaching and learning process of international students (de Witt, 2010), describing developments (Enders, 2004) or exploring strategies (Knight & de Witt, 1995). My primary motivation is to develop a framework of value that could be co-created between the various stakeholders (including the university, direct entry students and overseas partners). The successful outcome of this endeavour would support my role as an academic with responsibilities for direct entry students, by ascertaining the interventions that enhance the value of such programmes or moderate the threats and challenges identified.

Developing the story of my proposal. My experience of the proposal development stage for my first doctorate (PhD) and the professional doctorate are analogous in terms of presenting an idea and introducing theories, but that is where the similarity appears to end. For my PhD I was looking at practice as an 'outsider', while seeking theory to develop or test in context. I am now "inhabiting the hyphen" as described by Drake and Heath (2011, p. 21), through informing my practice as an 'insider', while attempting to conceptualise my research enquiry at a distance from my professional life.

Although I was aware of the 'direct entry issues' as a practitioner, I stepped out of the familiar in my professional setting to obtain a broader critical understanding and evaluation of British Higher and Further education. This led me to Tysome's (2004) findings of British education and training being ranked in the top five sectors, and generating export income (including educational publications, equipment and services) of over £13 billion. Various concerns relating to this endeavour were discussed in the findings, but were mainly in relation to quality issues in the internationalisation of higher education. With increasing international engagement in higher education between nations and regions (Marginson, 2010), I have similarly noted the increasing number of 'direct entry' students, where most would be international, as more UK HEIs are setting up their own overseas campuses and or are collaborating with overseas educational institutions.

As I attempt to connect the 'dots' (themes I have found from both readings and my experience as a practitioner), I will be looking forward to expanding my knowledge of how stakeholder interactions take place within higher education. By adopting Drake and Heath's (2011) 'insider-outsiderness' perspective, this would hopefully facilitate the identification of interventions that would improve the collaborative value between the stakeholders.

Since my doctoral proposal aims to theorise and contribute to new knowledge in the field of higher education, I have chosen an EdD to facilitate my transformational pilgrimage, where every step along the way will be laden with meaning (by way of enduring critical reflexivity) and witnessing change as new insights are provided and deeper understanding is attained.

CLOSING REFLECTIONS

The simple answer to the question 'Have we been there and done that?' is, of course, yes, since we are both already 'doctored' (Tennant, 2004). But as our respective reflective cases have shown, it is not quite as simple as that. To use the analogy of running a marathon: yes, we have already run a marathon before and so this means that we know we can do this, but, equally, we are aware of the preparation, training, stamina and sheer force of will entailed. Deciding to do a second – this time, professional – doctorate, is akin to choosing to run a second marathon in a different city – the distance is the same, but the course, the terrain, the crowd are certainly not.

As Tennant (2004, p. 435) has argued, the way in which universities now operate in response to the 'knowledge economy' has induced a profound shift in the role of the academic from an "independent, autonomous professional working within a disciplinary area in a collegial environment to the academic as corporate employed, delivering a high quality product to market". In response, universities have sought to evolve within this development and engage far more with the professions; hence the introduction of the professional doctorate in all its forms and focuses. Whilst as academics we are already professional researchers, we wish to actively engage in this profound shift ourselves by looking to become researching professionals. Yet whilst we would not go so far as to agree with Usher (2002) to say that this shift has, in turn, seen an epistemological concept of knowledge replaced by an economic one, it is true that the 'comportment' (Tennant, 2004, p. 435) of the traditional academic needs to be developed to reflect this change, and to respond to the new set of demands being placed on academics. As already 'doctored' (Tennant, 2004) academics whose professional community is a key component of the framework through which we are now looking to investigate as researching professionals, our position is therefore arguably rather different to many who choose to do a professional doctorate in education. However, through critically reflecting on our own and our community's professional practice, we hope that the professional doctorate will enable both a new mode of knowledge production as well as further develop our own academic 'comportment', giving us more strings to our bows, so to speak. From this perspective, the professional doctorate in education could actually be argued to be a pragmatic addition to our PhDs, namely, as advanced professional development for mid-career academics to gain a critically reflexive insight into our own and our field's practice.

To answer our titular question, our decisions to do a second, (professional) doctorate rest far less on the different epistemological spheres of knowledge production and far more on our personal needs to continue to develop as professional academics. Aspin (2007, p. 33) noted that we continue to learn by adopting a pragmatic "evolutionary epistemology" to make our own theories "meet for application, modification, and repair at every stage of our intellectual journey". This, however, requires more than passively acquiring generic research skills, but rather a form of learning that is more "consonant with the needs of civic participation and of agents capable of autonomously generating change for themselves" (Edwards, Ranson, & Strain, 2002, p. 527). To this end, the professional doctorate, and specifically the Doctorate of Education, since we are both engaged within the field of higher education, albeit in different disciplines, seemed the ideal framework through which to further our own professional development and, hopefully, as Scott (1995) noted, explicitly or implicitly change practice.

NOTES

[1] http://www.cambridgestudents.cam.ac.uk/your-course/examinations/graduate-exam-information/submitting-and-examination/phd-msc-mlitt
[2] Who, What, When, Where, Why (cf. http://its.unl.edu/bestpractices/remember-5-ws).
[3] See Taylor (2007), pp. 155–157 for an overview.

REFERENCES

Altbach, P., & Knight, J. (2007). The internationalization of higher education: Motivation and realities. *Journal of Studies in International Education, 11*, 290–305.

Andrade, M. S. (2006). International students in English-speaking universities. *Journal of Research in International Education, 5*(2), 131–154.

Aspin, D. N. (Ed.). (2007). *Philosophical perspectives on lifelong learning*. Dordrecht, The Netherlands: Springer.

Baird, J. R., Fensham, P. J., Gunstone, R. F., & White, R. T. (1991). The importance of reflection in improving science teaching and learning. *Journal of Research in Science Teaching, 28*(2), 163–182.

Baughan, J. (2004). Lessing and the Sturm und Drang: A reappraisal revisited. *The Modern Language Review, 99*(3), 827–828.

Bloom, B. S., Engelhart, M. D., Furst, E. J., Hill, W. H., & Kraftwohl, D. R. (1956). *Taxonomy of educational objectives: The classification of educational goals. Handbook I: Cognitive domain.* (p. 56). New York, NY: David McKay Company.

Bolton, G. (2005). *Reflective practice writing and professional development*. London: Sage.

Bourner, T., Katz, T., & Watson, D. (2000). Professional doctorates: The development of researching professionals. In T. Bourner, T. Katz, & D. Watson (Eds.), *New directions in professional higher education* (pp. 214–228). Buckingham, UK: Society for Research into Higher Education.

Bourner, T., Bowden, R., & Laing, S. (2001). Professional doctorates in England. *Studies in Higher Education, 26*(1), 65–83.

Brennan, M. (1995). Education doctorates: Reconstructing professional partnerships around research. *Australian Universities' Review, 2*, 20–22.

Canter, M. (2006). Foundation degrees: The development of best practice. *CEBE Transactions, 3*(1), 23–51.

Choi, B. C. K., & Pak, A. W. P. (2006). Multidisciplinarity, interdisciplinarity and transdisciplinarity in health research, services, education and policy: 1. Definitions, objectives and evidence of effectiveness. *Clinical and Investigative Medicine, 29*(6), 351–364.

Corney, M. (2003, February 2). *The future of higher education – a critical assessment of the HE* (White Paper. Policy Update No. 8). Norfolk, VA: Construction Industry Training Board.

Dewey, J. (1933). *How we think*. Lexington, MA: DC, Heath.

de Witt, H. (2010). *Internationalization of higher education in Europe, and its assessments, trends and issues*. Netherlands: Accreditation Organisation of the Netherlands and Flanders.

Drake, P., & Heath, L. (2011). *Practitioner research at doctoral level*. Routledge: Oxford.

Edwards, R., Ranson, S., & Strain, M. (2002). Reflexivity: Towards a theory of lifelong learning. *International Journal of Lifelong Education, 21*(6), 525–536.

Enders, J. (2004). Higher education, internationalisation, and the nation state: Recent developments and challenges to governance theory. *Higher Education, 47*(3), 361–382.

Fook, J. (2002). *Social work: Critical theory and practice*. London: Sage.

Gibbons, M., Limoges, C., Nowtny, H., Shwartzman, S., Scott, P., & Trow, M. (1994). *The new production of knowledge: The dynamics of science and research in contemporary societies*. London: Sage.

Gu, Q. (2010). Knowledge in context. Whose knowledge and for what context? In P. Thompson & M. Walker (Eds.), *The Routledge doctoral student's companion* (pp. 335–343). Routledge: Oxford.

Hajer, M. A. (1995). *The politics of ecological discourse: Ecological modernisation and the policy process*. Oxford: Clarendon Press.

Knight, J., & de Witt, H. (1995). Strategies for internationalisation of higher education: Historical and conceptual perspectives. In H. de Witt (Ed.), *A comparative study of Australia, Canada, Europe and the United States of America* (pp. 5–32). Amsterdam: European Association of International Education.

Kwiek, M. (2003). The state, the market and higher education, challenges for the new century. In M. Kwiek (Ed.), *The university, globalisation and central Europe* (pp. 71–114). Frankfurt & New York, NY: Peter Lang.

Lunt, I. (2006). *Professional doctorates and their contribution to professional development and careers* (ESRC Full Research Report, R000223643). Swindon: Economic and Social Research Council

Lyotard, J-F. (1979). *La condition postmoderne: rapport sur le savoir*. Paris: Les Éditions de Minuit.

Marginson, S. (2010). Higher education in the global knowledge economy. *Procedia Social and Behavioral Sciences, 2*, 6962–6980.

Maxwell, T. W., & Shanahan, P. J. (1997). Towards a reconceptualization of the doctorate: Issues arising from comparative data relating to the EdD degree in Australia, *Studies in Higher Education, 22*(2), 133–150.

McWilliam, E., & James, R. (2002). Doctoral education in a knowledge economy. *Higher Education Research and Development, 21*(2), 100–117.

Noble, K. A. (1994). *Changing doctoral degrees: An international perspective*. Buckingham: Society for Research into Higher Education and Open University Press.

Qiang, A. (2003). Internationalization of higher education: Towards a conceptual framework. *Policy Futures in Education, 1*(2), 248–270.

Quality Assurance Agency. (2008). *The framework for higher education qualifications in England, Wales and Northern Ireland*. Gloucester: QAA. Retrieved January 5, 2016, from www.qaa.ac.uk/Publications/InformationAndGuidance/Pages/The-framework-for-highereducation-qualifications-in-England-Wales-and-Northern-Ireland.aspx

Schön, D. A. (1983). *The reflective practitioner*. London, Temple Smith.

Scott, D., Brown, A., Lunt, I., & Thorne, L. (2004). *Professional doctorates : Integrating professional and academic knowledge*. Maidenhead: Society for Research into Higher Education & Open University Press.

Scott, P. (1995). *The meanings of mass higher education.* Buckingham: Society for Research in HE and Open University Press.

Taylor, A. (2007). Learning to become researching professionals: The case of the doctorate of education. *International Journal of Teaching and Learning in Higher Education, 19*(2), 154–166.

Tennant, M. (2004). Doctoring the knowledge worker. *Studies in Continuing Education, 26*(3), 431–441.

Thomson, P., & Walker, M. (2010a). Doctoral education in context. The changing nature of the doctorate and doctoral students. In P. Thompson & M. Walker (Eds.), *The Routledge doctoral student's companion* (pp. 9–26). London: Routledge.

Thomson, P., & Walker, M. (2010b). Last words. Why doctoral study? In P. Thompson & M. Walker (Eds.), *The Routledge doctoral student's companion* (pp. 390–402). Routledge: Oxford.

Tysome, T. (2004, April 23). UK market worth £10 billion. *Times Higher Education Supplement* (UK Council for Graduate Education). Retrieved January 4, 2015, from http://ukcge.ac.uk/

Usher, R. (2002). A diversity of doctorates: Fitness for the knowledge economy? *Higher Education Research & Development, 21*(2), 143–153.

Wilson, T. (2002). *Strangers to ourselves: Discovering the adaptive unconsciousness.* Cambridge, MA: The Belkap Press of Harvard University Press.

SIMON DOWLING

4. THREE AGENDAS FOR RESEARCHING PROFESSIONALS

Challenging and Developing Your Thinking about
Your Doctoral Practices

INTRODUCTION

Aims

This chapter considers the 'positioning' of researching professionals who are
funded by the organisation to which they belong and which they are researching,
as I am. Griffiths (1998, p. 133) suggests that all researchers need to engage in
reflexive examination of their own socio-political positions and interests because
"bias comes not from having ethical and political positions – that is inevitable
– but from not acknowledging them". Reflexive self-examination has helped
me to understand that my struggle with my own positioning is due in part to the
multiple identities in tension with each other that I have come to occupy. Drawing
on the methodological and empirical literatures, and on my experiences as both
a professional (a school teacher) and a doctoral student, I suggest three critical
agendas through which to consider reflexive practice and positioning. My proposed
agendas address: (1) researching professionals' positioning as simultaneous
'insider' and 'outsider'; (2) the kinds of knowledge that they can produce; and
(3) ethical challenges that they face when being funded. These sets of issues will
resonate with all doctoral students whose journey is funded, not only with those
undertaking professional doctorates.

Background

Universities have become part of the globalised knowledge economy (Loxley &
Seery, 2012; Taylor, 2007). This has produced an increasing emphasis on context-
specific and problem-oriented knowledge creation (Lang et al., 2012). Several
U.K. universities have responded to these imperatives by adding new doctoral
education formats to their 'traditional' PhD-by-thesis, including practice-based or
'professional doctorates', 'new route' PhDs, and doctorates by publication (Wildy,
Peden, & Chan, 2014). 'Professional doctorates' are research degrees designed for

P. Burnard et al. (Eds.), Transformative Doctoral Research Practices for Professionals, 43–60.

practitioners which combine research training via a taught programme and research in the workplace, and have the aims of making a difference to the profession and of directly influencing the working lives of the practitioners (Taylor, 2007). In England, researching professionals most commonly self-fund their courses, but may be funded in whole or in part by employers (Mellors-Bourne, Robinson, & Metcalfe, 2016), or possibly by other sponsors such as a research council (McCay, 2010). I took up the opportunity to study for a professional doctorate in education (EdD) because my head teacher (principal) believed that the school, the wider profession, and I personally would all benefit. He agreed to fund my course if I focused my research on the specific context of my school's work in leading a new multi-school collaborative improvement initiative. A critical question that this arrangement has raised for me is to what extent it exemplifies the practice-oriented purpose and research focus that professional doctorate programmes have been designed to produce (Mellors-Bourne, Robinson, & Metcalfe, 2016), and at the same time to what extent it places my doctoral research practices under methodological and ethical pressures. It is these pressures that my reflexive agendas are intended to address.

Three Agendas for Researching Professionals

In this chapter, I propose three 'agendas' through which researching professionals can challenge and develop their own thinking about their doctoral research practices:

One. Being simultaneously an 'insider' (a working member of the organisation being studied, or 'emic') and an 'outsider' (a researcher seeking to uncover detailed information about the organisation, or 'etic') (Morris, Leung, Ames, & Lickel, 1999), researching professionals seem to occupy positions which threaten to undermine the validity of their research in both ethical and practical terms.

Two. The knowledge that researching professionals seek to produce, and the contribution to practice that they might make, can be thought of as being influenced by the various and sometimes conflicting purposes of undertaking their research (Taylor, 2007).

Three. An additional layer of ethical challenges faces researching professionals whose work is funded by the organisation that they are studying (Anderson et al., 2012; Miller, Moore, & Strang, 2006). I suggest that being funded raises ethical challenges in four dimensions:

- *obligation* – the pressure to produce particular outcomes which is generated by the expectations of the funder;
- *power* relationships with the research participants;

- consequent problems in securing the *authenticity* of the participants' voices;
- the student's own disposition and assumptions as a member of the organisation being studied, leading to *predictive* thinking.

Reflexivity

The literature of doctoral research practice predominantly offers reflexivity as a fundamental element in developing oneself as a researcher. Kamler and Thomson (2014, p. 75) define "a reflexive scholar [as] one who applies to their own work the same critical stance, the same interrogative questions, and the same refusal to take things for granted as they do with their research data". In this chapter, I apply the idea of the 'reflexive scholar' to practitioners who research their own organisations. In this context, being a reflexive scholar means that researching professionals need to recognise and interrogate their fluid positioning as they move between the communities of the academy and the workplace (Drake & Heath, 2011; Mercer, 2007). I suggest that a key reflexive step is to analyse critically one's own subjective points of view (that is, experiences of and insights into the subject of study that are personal to the researcher, and which may be tacit rather than explicit), so as to identify and acknowledge the perhaps unresolvable tensions between research and professional priorities. It follows that a key product of these tensions is the 'situatedness' of ethics for professionals who research their own workplaces. The fair and faithful representation of the research subject, which is also the researcher's own professional community, must inevitably be influenced by the various positions that the researcher occupies. Thus, given that the researching professional, as with the ethnographer or anthropologist, "in part creates the facts that he or she then records" (Gobo, 2008, p. 73), reflexive consideration of how and why the resulting picture is being produced by the researcher is a vital part of the representation process. By means of the following agendas, I would like to offer some transformative practices which could help researching professionals to interrogate their own positioning, thereby "think[ing] and act[ing] critically about the principles and practice of research" (Taylor, 2007, p. 160).

AGENDA ONE – POSITIONING YOURSELF AS A
RESEARCHING PROFESSIONAL

My first agenda deals with three items: (1) researching professionals' membership identity; (2) the difficulty of maintaining a 'critical distance' when researching one's own workplace; and (3) dealing with the intimate knowledge that is accessible to a researching professional.

I am an embodiment of my first agenda: a full-time practitioner (a school teacher) and also a part-time doctoral student researching the influence of a collaborative group of schools on teachers' professional development. Researching professionals are in a uniquely privileged position as members of the organisation, or participants in the process, that they are studying. Such an 'insider researcher' "possesses intimate knowledge" of "the community and its members" (Hellawell, 2006, p. 483) that form the subject of enquiry, in ways that are denied to external researchers. This intimacy is clearly an advantage in terms of access to and cultural understanding of the subject organisation. But at the same time, there are significant "hidden ethical and methodological dimensions of insiderness" (Labaree, 2002, p. 109) which demand that a researching professional be especially reflexive. I therefore formulated critical questions to interrogate the ways in which my positions and identities could distort or prejudice what I looked for, how I looked for it, and my representation of what I might find.

Item 1. Membership Identity

The first item on this agenda is the 'membership identity' of researching professionals. Their position is both *emic* (as a professional member of the organisation being studied) and also *etic* (as a doctoral researcher seeking to draw generally applicable conclusions from the particular culture being studied) (Morris, Leung, Ames, & Lickel, 1999). They are thus located in at least two communities of practice (Wenger, 1998), their workplace and their doctoral course at university, and these communities may have different values, assumptions and priorities. In the case of education, I have detected tension between the two communities in that many school teachers do not regard the work of educational researchers as relevant on a day-to-day basis to their own practice. This dichotomy has been entrenched by recent changes to initial teacher education (ITE) in England which position teaching as a technical craft, place it in a marketised and performative context, and see ITE as largely a matter of practice acquisition (Brown, Rowley, & Smith, 2016). A gap in perceptions of the value of research activity has been found in a range of professions including education, social work and medicine (Hammersley, 2001; Bellamy et al., 2013; Greenhalgh, Howick, & Maskrey, 2014). Thus, critical questions to ask here were whether I valued my research activity more highly than did my workplace colleagues, on whose co-operation I depended to conduct my research; and what effect that difference would have on my practices.

Insider researchers may find it easier to recruit participants for their research because they can make a request through established and trusted channels that are not open to an external researcher. But the research relationship is complicated by the fluid or 'dynamic' position that the researcher occupies in the workplace, a blend of involvement and detachment which may vary in time and space (Mullings, 1999). For example, someone who has formal authority at work over people who agree to participate in the project faces a substantial challenge when moving into the position of researcher. Could responses to the project, including agreement to take part at all, be said, with confidence, to be free of the influence of the workplace relationship? It has been argued that insider research must therefore be regarded as socially shaped (Loxley & Seery, 2008), but clearly there are dangers in using a research framework in which concepts and culture are shared by the researcher and all members of the project sample. Due to practical and ethical concerns uncovered by reflexive questioning, I decided not to include my own school in my sample, and I did not have any previous direct relationship with the schools that I did include. In this way, I attempted to develop and maintain a 'critical distance' between my simultaneous *emic* and *etic* positions (that is, to put aside prior assumptions and tacit understandings which were based on my own professional experience) (Appleby, 2013). The issue of 'critical distance' is considered under the second item on this agenda, which I discuss in the next section.

Item 2. Difficulty of Maintaining a 'Critical Distance'

A question raised about research conducted by researching professionals is whether they can achieve sufficient 'critical distance' from their workplace and colleagues to produce valid and reliable evidence about them (Drake & Heath, 2011; Sikes & Potts, 2008). Conversely, the ethnographic and anthropological research traditions favour the observer's 'participation' in the target culture on a spectrum of degrees of immersion (Spradley, 1980; Delamont, 2004). In some professional settings that are not comparable to those commonly studied by ethnographers and anthropologists, a limited 'negotiated interactive observer' position may be more acceptable to participants than full or partial immersion (Wind, 2008).

Although 'critical distance' might be achieved at the moment when analysis is carried out, it does not appear possible for researching professionals, who are always members of their organisations, to occupy permanently a non-participatory position. It may therefore be helpful to think of position in relative terms, as on a continuum. Some people are 'relative insiders', and some are 'relative outsiders', depending on their and on others' perceptions of their membership identity (Griffiths, 1998). Thus a researching professional who maintains effective relationships with work colleagues while also accessing their (possibly shared) experiences for research purposes could be thought of as a 'relative insider'. A researching professional whose research activity is regarded with some suspicion by colleagues, possibly because they believe it to be a form of management snooping, could be seen as a 'relative outsider'. But no position is comfortable for the researching professional. Relative insiders may face the charge of being too distanced from the workplace community of which they are part: they have found a voice for themselves, but it may not be the voice of others in the community. They may be accused of selling out to the norms of university-based academic research. Relative outsiders may face charges of exploiting the workplace community, of hijacking the voices of its members, or of strengthening stereotypes (Griffiths, 1998). Critical questions to ask under this item include interrogating how events, conceptual categories, and assumptions on the part of both the participants and the researcher, might have been produced by particular institutional practices, values and cultures.

Researching professionals could perhaps take solace from the view that it is the task of insider research to identify such socio-political and historical factors which influence practice; to open up issues of values; to integrate the professional with the personal (both for the researcher and for the subjects of research); and to be educative for all participants (Reed & Proctor, 1995). From this perspective, the researching professional's position may be seen as productive rather than limiting, in that these research aims cannot readily be achieved by someone entering the field from the outside: being part of the organisation and its processes is essential to understanding the case. 'Intimate knowledge' gained in this way is the third item on this agenda, which I deal with in the next section.

Item 3. Intimate Knowledge

It has been argued that a researcher's lack of knowledge of the history and culture of the particular organisation under study should be made part of the critique of external research more often than it is (Smyth & Holian, 2008). Concerns over the practical and ethical tensions of insider research can be balanced with the unusually privileged access that the researcher has as a member of the workplace community. There may be difficulties in negotiating exactly which parts of the organisation (people, operations, information) may be investigated, but insiders are in a position to use knowledge that they already have, such as awareness of organisational priorities and existing channels of communication, to pursue these negotiations (Brannick & Coghlan, 2007).

But the professional burden of 'insiderness', in this respect, is 'guilty knowledge' (Williams, 2010). This term means any knowledge that a researcher has that may do another person harm. If the researcher recognises that harm may arise, then an appropriate ethical assessment can be made, leading to a decision about confidentiality. A more complex instance could arise if the researcher acquires knowledge which has significance that the participant and the researcher are unaware of. Examples might include self-compromised anonymity, where participants unintentionally render their identities detectable; and courting professional risk, when participants voice their own concerns which the researcher does not recognise as detrimental to their standing in the organisation. Potential damage caused by such 'guilty knowledge' can be revealed through critical reflection on the part of the researcher, possibly using intimate knowledge of the community to weigh professional judgements against research judgements (Dobson, 2009), and in some instances allowing the former to trump the latter. Key questions that might help to address and balance these two lenses include: 'In whose interests am I asking this question?', 'Who might be damaged by this information and how?' and 'How can I represent work colleagues' experiences and views both accurately and without detriment to them?'

I have shown these three items under Agenda One in Figure 1 below:

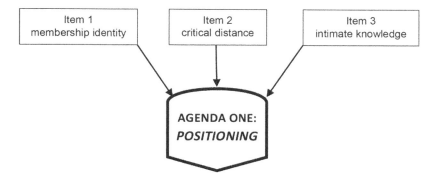

Figure 1. Agenda One: The researching professional's positioning

The three items in boxes are used to suggest that the positioning of researching professionals is influenced by their membership identity (of at least two communities of practice); by the difficulty of maintaining 'critical distance' between their work as researchers and their subjects of study (which are their professional workplaces); and by the intimate knowledge of their organisations that being an 'insider' entails.

The types of knowledge that researching professionals have, acquire or create by virtue of their multiple positions need to be subjected to reflexive scrutiny. This challenge is addressed in Agenda Two, which is discussed next.

AGENDA TWO – PRODUCING KNOWLEDGE FOR VARIOUS PURPOSES

The focus of a professional doctorate is usually on a problem or activity, customer base or community with which the student is already familiar through working in or with it, with the aims of understanding it better (that is, to create knowledge), and of effecting improvement to how it works (that is, to contribute positively to practice) (Taylor, 2007). The kinds of knowledge that are valued for these purposes are considered in the following items under Agenda Two.

Item 1. Modes of Knowledge Generation

Researching professionals may have assumptions and ideas about what they expect to find out based on their experience as practitioners (Drake & Heath, 2011). This approach to enquiry influences the type or 'mode' of knowledge that they can produce. While Mode One knowledge is seen traditionally to reside in discrete disciplines focused in universities, Mode Two knowledge is seen to be trans-disciplinary and generated through practice or experience (Gibbons et al., 1994). The knowledge that researching professionals may produce, founded on or responding to what they already know about their workplace, is thus more closely aligned to the 'new', practice-oriented Mode Two than the 'traditional', university-oriented Mode One. But as doctoral *students*, researching professionals face the problem of also satisfying the particular demands of the academy in how they formulate and present the knowledge that they produce, so as to qualify for doctoral status. They must "transform their existing models of professional knowledge and replace them with a critical and analytic reflection" (Drake & Heath, 2011, p. 18).

This key academic demand could be approached by paying attention to further modes of knowledge which the researching professional is producing, but which might otherwise remain unspoken or even unconscious. Scott et al. (2004) have proposed that 'professional doctorates' suggest four modes of knowledge in all: in addition to Modes One and Two, they identify Mode Three, centred on conscious deliberation and reflection about the topic of study by the individual student, which is non-teachable; and Mode Four, centred on the development of the individual through the critical, self-interrogative practice of reflexivity. Mode Four chimes with the personal development, general intellectual interest and career advancement identified as reasons for undertaking a doctorate (Leonard, Becker, & Coate, 2005; Gill & Hoppe, 2009). It thus appears that researching professionals are likely to value knowledge about themselves as a key element of the knowledge that their projects create. If this self-investigation is framed reflexively and foregrounded in the project's outcomes, then it could be used to satisfy the common academic requirement for critical reflection in professional doctorates (Boud & Walker, 1998; Lucas, 2012). Critical questions to use here might include: 'Which assumptions and positions deriving from my professional experience have led me to ask certain questions and not others?', 'How has my framing of my analysis influenced the knowledge that I have produced?' and 'What are the possible misunderstandings of my data that my own assumptions and positions might cause?' The positioning of individual researching professionals seems to be key to the knowledge that they can produce. I discuss the connected issue of how their research projects are oriented under the following item.

Item 2. Orientations of Research Outcomes

For the theoretical perspectives on knowledge production considered under Item 1 to be transformative to the doctoral student who is juggling professional and academic careers, they need to be seen in the light of each individual student's situation. For example, in reflecting on the modes of knowledge that my own research project might create, I had to consider the different 'orientations' of my project (Noffke, 1997; Rearick & Feldman, 1999).

Firstly, it was *situation-oriented* in that my focus was on a specific case, and one aim of the project was to make recommendations for action to the case organisation's leaders. The knowledge that would be valued for this purpose had a strongly local and instrumental bias towards the 'real world' in 'real time' (Costley, 2013).

Dissemination was in the form of relatively brief reports delivered exclusively to the organisation's leaders, headed by an executive summary with a small number of targeted recommendations, and including a brief discussion of my survey findings. The leaders then chose to act or not act on my recommendations in the light of local priorities.

Secondly, my project was *policy-oriented* because I undertook a critique of a national-level school improvement policy, basing my judgements on one instance of the policy in action. It was possible, if only remotely, that policy changes might ensue from the dissemination of my research. In this orientation, dissemination was publicly in print and online; by presentation at conferences and other meetings of education professionals; and in non-specialist form such as industry magazines and social media platforms. My contribution to knowledge in this orientation was to a widely-distributed, opinion-based debate that might influence policy-making (Lomas, 1997; Alexander, 2014).

Thirdly, my project was *theory-oriented* in that a major requirement of my doctorate was to generate knowledge that could be expressed as theory, not merely to report the empirical observations from which that theory was drawn. I had therefore to relate my specific case to the wider academic literature and to other examples of the case. The theory orientation is primarily academic, and so the means of dissemination in this instance was by doctoral thesis (Bourner, Bowden, & Laing, 2001). I did not expect the readership of the full-length work to be wide; for the theory generated by my research to have significant impact, it needed to be extracted from the thesis, slimmed down, and published in other, more widely accessible formats (Kamler, 2008) including some of those listed under my discussion above of policy-oriented outcomes.

To summarise Agenda Two, I suggest that researching professionals should ask critical questions about the types of knowledge that their research can produce. Questions might include: 'How is knowledge production being influenced in both content and dissemination practices by the various orientations or purposes that my research has?' and 'What unexpected or under-valued modes of knowledge could I develop?'

I have shown the items discussed under Agenda Two in Figure 2 below:

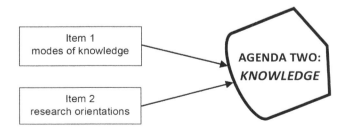

Figure 2. Agenda Two: Knowledge produced by a researching professional

The two items in boxes are used to suggest that the knowledge content that researching professionals can produce is influenced by the modes that are open to them, including knowledge which responds to or is founded on an individual's professional experiences. The formats in which knowledge is conveyed and the means of its dissemination into the 'real world' are influenced by the orientations that the research project might have.

The knowledge that researching professionals whose course is funded can produce is also influenced by a layer of ethical challenge, which I discuss in the following section under Agenda Three.

AGENDA THREE – ETHICAL CHALLENGES TO THE FUNDED RESEARCHING PROFESSIONAL

My own position as a researching professional is ethically complex in that my doctoral course has been funded by the organisation to which I belong, and which is the subject of my research project. Based on interviews with higher education researchers, Williams (2010, p. 257) warns that "advice to resort to criteria for well-designed research methodology ... fails to offer protection from ethical complexity ... Not far beneath the surface of such advice lies a reef of instrumentalist risk-benefit ethics". In reflecting on the ethical pitfalls of insider research in my own context, I identified four dimensions where bias or distortion could occur if I was insufficiently reflexive in my approach. What follows is a discussion of my experience in each of these dimensions, where I foreground my own dilemmas and detail the responses that I made. I do not claim to have found definitive solutions to these challenges, but I suggest that funded doctoral students may find that my experience chimes with theirs, and that reflexive attention to these issues is an essential element in navigating the 'ethical reef' that Williams identifies.

Item 1. The Obligation Dimension

I was a senior teacher in the school which led the organisation (a voluntary, collaborative, multi-school improvement group) that was the subject of my doctoral project. I had the support of my head teacher, who also formally headed the organisation. With the agreement of the 'steering group' of senior leaders which directed the organisation, he had authority to pay my doctoral course fees from the organisation's funds because my project was seen as a key element of the organisation's self-evaluation process. I was expected to research the effectiveness of the organisation and to report back periodically to the steering group, and was accountable to that body, so there was a sense in which I was bound to and by its leadership. I was indeed grateful for the opportunity to do a doctoral degree which I would not otherwise be able to undertake.

These pressures might be conceptualised as an obligation dimension to my research. I could be criticised for apparently producing findings which aligned with what the organisation's leaders thought needed to be said about the organisation's work – in effect, to tell them what they wanted to hear (Rossman & Rallis, 2012, p. 58) – because I felt obliged to them for funding my project. In discussions with my head teacher before enrolling on the doctoral course, he assured me that he did not expect an endorsement of the organisation's work, but would prefer an unvarnished, 'warts and all' account because it would be more genuinely and usefully evaluative for the leadership group's purposes. However, 'evaluation' was not *my* primary aim in designing my project: my aim was to produce valid research leading to the award of my EdD degree. This is an instance of the potential clash of perspectives created by different reasons for codifying and disseminating knowledge: the organisation's leaders saw me as an 'individual expert' whose research could be appropriated to their particular purposes (Lam, 1997). The question of knowledge ownership is thus closely implicated in my first item on obligation. Critical questions to ask here might include 'Who expects what of my project's outcomes?' and 'Who owns the knowledge that I am producing?'

The second item on this agenda addresses the power that a researcher may appear to have by virtue of being funded, which I discuss in the following section.

Item 2. The Power Dimension

Research in relation to practice may be compromised by significant power relations. The 'authorised' nature of my project, meaning that it had organisational approval and permission, raised the question of whether participants in my research would feel that they needed to respond in particular ways, or even that they were compelled to take part at all, because I might be taken to represent the organisation's leadership – a power dimension (Berger, 2013).

Reflexivity is a necessary counter to this threat because it "also means interrogating how we might be perpetuating particular kinds of power relationships, be advancing particular ways of naming and discussing people, experiences and events" (Kamler & Thomson, 2014, p. 75). I suggest that researching professionals need to be on constant alert for both overt and covert manifestations of power, and particularly so when funded by the organisation they are studying. Critical questions to use here might include 'What is the participant's professional relationship to me?', 'How does power circulate in that relationship?' and 'In what ways could power relationships affect what participants choose to say?' This approach to reflexivity is indeed uncomfortable, or 'dangerous', because it demands attention to the participants themselves and to the issues that are important to them, not just to methodology and processes (Pillow, 2010).

The issue of securing participants' authentic voices is considered under the third item on this agenda, which I discuss next.

Item 3. The Authenticity Dimension

In designing my project, I was highly conscious of the need to secure responses as free as possible from bias and distortion caused by power relationships or other positional threats (Kvale, 2006), thus following the well-understood ethical path of vigilance to ensure the authenticity of participants' voices (Denzin & Lincoln, 2000). However, given the unknowable threat of 'guilty knowledge' discussed above under Agenda One, Item 3, could commonly-employed ethical precautions to secure participants' informed consent, to avoid detriment and to ensure privacy (BERA, 2011) be sufficient?

In connection with the ethical dimension of power relationships discussed under Item 2 above, the issue of deception would arise if, in attempting to reduce the influence of power, I did not fully identify myself and my position(s) to my participants (Griffiths, 1998). Concerned about this problem, and also in order to foster a collaborative atmosphere where openness was likely to thrive (Anderson & Anuka, 2003), I took the decision during the course of the interview phase to reveal a little more about myself (such as my workplace and job title, and my reasons for undertaking the project) than I had originally intended. This did not seem to alarm any interviewee, but led in most cases to an extended discussion of the topics at hand (James & Busher, 2006). I judged that a more open atmosphere was in tune with the values underpinning my research approach, a 'situated' ethical judgement that I believed I could justify because it promoted the authenticity of participants' voices.

A fourth dimension of ethical challenge to the professional doctoral researcher, that of falling prey to assumptions and preconceptions about the workplace situation, is dealt with in the following section.

Item 4. The Prediction Dimension

Given that I was researching in a familiar setting, I faced the threat of a possibly unacknowledged theoretical stance at the start of the project (Drake & Heath, 2011). This could be conceptualised as a predictive dimension – I could find what I was tacitly looking for or expected to see (Guba, 1981; Shenton, 2004).

My own disposition as a middle-level leader is towards the distributed and collaborative end of the leadership style spectrum. After more than 20 years in teaching, I am rather sceptical of centralised or top-down, 'hierarchical' initiatives for educational improvement (Fullan, 2001; Fielding et al., 2005). How would these values that I have as a practitioner shape or bias my approach as a researcher, even if they contradicted the obligation that I might feel to the organisation's leaders who agreed to fund my course (as discussed above under Item 1 in this agenda)? My sceptical stance, or pre-disposition to be disappointed, might have appeared to be a sufficiently critical position to adopt: I would not automatically assume that because something is new, it must be better than what has existed before. However, was there a danger in going too far in the opposite direction and expecting an innovation to fail? Remaining neutral in the prediction dimension was probably impossible to achieve.

Kamler and Thomson (2014) propose that an acceptable response to the threat posed by predictive thinking is actively to use the first person to locate the researcher in the research. The various theoretical and dispositional influences on the researcher's stance, which might otherwise remain hidden, can thus be voiced. For example, I needed to state explicitly that "I favour a collaborative perspective in my own professional life". I could then acknowledge that this disposition would influence my understanding of the data that I collected. Further, such a practice would make the researcher's contribution to knowledge original, because the particular angle that an individual takes on a research problem constitutes the locus of originality (Dunleavy, 2003). This appears to be a transformative practice of particular utility to researching professionals: the tensions caused by the multiplicity of positions, purposes and ethical challenges that they face can be foregrounded and acknowledged, even if they cannot ultimately be resolved.

Agenda Three raises a layer of ethical challenges for researching professionals who are funded by the organisations that they are studying. I have shown these four ethical dimensions in the diagram below:

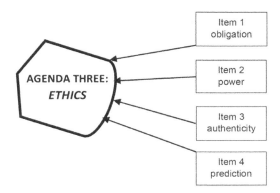

Figure 3. Agenda Three: Ethical challenges to funded research

The four items in boxes are used to suggest that researching professionals face several dimensions of ethical challenge, particularly if they are funded by the organisation that they are studying. There are significant problems to deal with in the dimensions of obligation to funders, power relationships with research participants, securing the participants' authentic voices, and being reflexively aware of the assumptions and preconceptions that influence their thinking.

CLOSING REFLECTIONS: TRANSFORMATIVE PRACTICES FOR GRANT- OR
ORGANISATIONALLY-FUNDED RESEARCHING PROFESSIONALS

The complex challenges faced by researching professionals mean that they need to incorporate constant reflexive checking into their doctoral practice as a means of transforming their research design and outcomes. I offer the following checklist, based both on the methodological and empirical literatures and on my own experience as a researching professional whose course is funded by the organisation that I am studying:

Agenda One: Positioning Yourself as a Researching Professional

1.1. Which communities of practice do you belong to? What tensions and conflicts could be felt as you move between your communities?
1.2. How far can you, and should you, maintain a critical distance between you and your subject of study?
1.3. How can you, and should you, use your intimate knowledge of the organisation to weigh professional judgements against research judgements?

Agenda Two: Producing Knowledge for Various Purposes

2.1. What different modes of knowledge are you able, or do you want, to produce, and who values which outputs?
2.2. What are the dissemination orientations of your research project? What tensions could arise between them?

Agenda Three: Navigating Ethical Challenges to the Funded Researching Professional

3.1. Do you face an obligation to your funder? What expectations are there?
3.2. Are there power relationships with your research participants to navigate?
3.3. How can you secure your participants' authentic voices in your research?
3.4. What are your theoretical and dispositional assumptions that might cause you to engage in predictive thinking?

These agendas are brought together, with the researching professional ('RP') at the centre, in the composite diagram shown below in Figure 4.

This diagram uses the ideas and practices discussed in this chapter to suggest that researching professionals may find themselves surrounded by a number of threats to or pressures on their research practices. They can transform their doctoral research practices by paying constant reflexive attention to: (1) their fluid and possibly conflicting positioning in their communities; (2) the types of knowledge that they can produce and the reasons why different types may be valued; and (3) the ethical challenges that they face as 'insider' researchers who may be funded

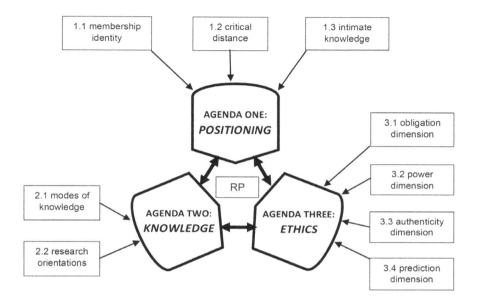

Figure 4. Three agendas for funded researching professionals

by the organisation that they are studying. For example, I struggled with the issue of how much to reveal to participants about my membership identities in relation to my research on the multi-school group that funded my course. I decided to be open about the authorisation of my project because that seemed more honest, even if the revelation of a power relationship might produce distortion in participants' responses. The outcomes of reflexive self-interrogation may be uncomfortable both personally and methodologically, but that is all the more reason to engage in the practice. A professional doctorate student in education has claimed that, "Through constant practices of surfacing and questioning hitherto underlying and taken for granted … assumptions, … concepts which I had hitherto considered stable, unitary and certain were made permeable, fragmented and less predictable" (Forbes, 2008, p. 457). I suggest that this is a positive state for researching professionals and indeed for all doctoral students to reach: I hope that my proposed agendas can assist in the journey towards it.

REFERENCES

Alexander, R. (2014). The best that has been thought and said? *Forum, 56*(1), 157–166.
Anderson, E., Solomon, S., Heitman, E., DuBois, J., Fisher, C., Kost, R., Lawless, M., Ramsey, C., Jones, B., Ammerman, A., & Ross, L. (2012). Research ethics education for community-engaged research: A review and research agenda. *Journal of Empirical Research on Human Research Ethics, 7*(2), 3–19.
Anderson, T., & Anuka, H. (2003). *e-Research: Methods, strategies and issues.* Boston, MA: Ablongman.

Appleby, M. (2013). he nature of practitioner research: Critical distance, power and ethics. *Practitioner Research in Higher Education, 7*(1), 11–21.

Bellamy, J., Mullen, E., Satterfield, J., Newhouse, R., Ferguson, M., Brownson, R., & Spring, B. (2013). Implementing evidence-based practice education in social work: A transdisciplinary approach. *Research on Social Work Practice, 23*(4), 426–436.

British Educational Research Association (BERA). (2011). *Ethical guidelines for educational research.* London: BERA.

Berger, R. (2013, January 3). Now I see it, now I don't: Researcher's position and reflexivity in qualitative research. *Qualitative Research, 15*(2), 219–234. Retrieved February 2, 2013, from http://qrj.sagepub.com/content/early/2013/01/03/1468794112468475

Boud, D., & Walker, D. (1998). Promoting reflection in professional courses: The challenge of context. *Studies in Higher Education, 23*(2), 191–206.

Bourner, T., Bowden, R., & Laing, S. (2001). Professional doctorates in England. *Studies in Higher Education, 26*(1), 65–83.

Brannick, T., & Coghlan, D. (2007). In defense of being "native": The case for insider academic research. *Organizational Research Methods, 10*(1), 59–74.

Brown, T., Rowley, H., & Smith, K. (2016, March). *The beginnings of school led teacher training: New challenges for university teacher education* (School Direct Research Project Final Report). Manchester: Manchester Metropolitan University.

Costley, C. (2013). Evaluation of the current status and knowledge contributions of professional doctorates. *Quality in Higher Education, 19*(1), 7–27.

Delamont, S. (2004). Ethnography and participant observation. In C. Seale, G. Gobo, J. F. Gubrium, & D. Silverman (Eds.), *Qualitative research practice* (pp. 205–217). London: Sage.

Denzin, N., & Lincoln, Y. (Eds.). (2000). *Handbook of qualitative research* (2nd ed.). London: Sage.

Dobson, R. (2009). 'Insiderness', 'involvement' and emotions: Impacts for methods, 'knowledge' and social research. *People, Place & Policy Online, 3*(3), 183–195.

Drake, P., & Heath, L. (2011). *Practitioner research at doctoral level: Developing coherent research methodologies.* Abingdon: Routledge.

Dunleavy, P. (2003). *Authoring a PhD: How to plan, draft, write and finish a doctoral thesis or dissertation.* London: Palgrave.

Fielding, M., Bragg, S., Craig, J., Cunningham, I., Eraut, M., Gillinson, S., Horne, M., Robinson, C., & Thorp, J. (2005). *Factors influencing the transfer of good practice, RR615.* Nottingham: Department for Education and Skills.

Forbes, J. (2008). Reflexivity in professional doctoral research. *Reflective Practice, 9*(4), 449–460.

Fullan, M. (2001). *The new meaning of educational change* (3rd ed.). New York, NY: Teachers College Press.

Gibbons, M., Limoges, C., Nowotny, H., Schwartzman, S., Scott, P., & Trow, M. (1994). *The new production of knowledge: The dynamics of science and research in contemporary societies.* London: Sage.

Gill, T., & Hoppe, U. (2009). The business professional doctorate as an informing channel: A survey and analysis. *International Journal of Doctoral Studies, 4*, 27–57.

Gobo, G. (2008). *Doing ethnography.* London: Sage.

Greenhalgh, T, Howick, J., & Maskrey, N. (2014). Evidence based medicine: A movement in crisis? *British Medical Journal, 348.* Retrieved February 3, 2016, www.bmj.com/content/348/bmj.g3725.full

Griffiths, M. (1998). *Educational research for social justice: Getting off the fence.* Buckingham: Open University Press.

Guba, E. (1981). Criteria for assessing the trustworthiness of naturalistic inquiries. *Educational Communication and Technology Journal, 29*, 75–91.

Hammersley, M. (2001, September). *Some questions about evidence-based practice in education.* Paper presented at the Annual Conference of the British Educational Research Association, University of Leeds, England.

Hellawell, D. (2006). Inside–out: Analysis of the insider–outsider concept as a heuristic device to develop reflexivity in students doing qualitative research. *Teaching in Higher Education, 11*(4), 483–494.

James, N., & Busher, H. (2006). Credibility, authenticity and voice: Dilemmas in online interviewing. *Qualitative Research, 6*(3), 403–420.

Kamler, B. (2008). Rethinking doctoral publication practices: Writing from and beyond the thesis. *Studies in Higher Education, 33*(3), 283–294.

Kamler, B., & Thomson, P. (2014). *Helping doctoral students write: Pedagogies for supervision* (2nd ed.). Abingdon: Routledge.

Kvale, S. (2006). Dominance through interviews and dialogues. *Qualitative Inquiry, 12*(3), 480–500.

Labaree, R. (2002). The risk of 'going observationalist': Negotiating the hidden dilemmas of being an insider participant observer. *Qualitative Research, 2*(1), 97–122.

Lam, A. (1997). Embedded firms, embedded knowledge: Problems of collaboration and knowledge transfer in global co-operative ventures. *Organization Studies, 18*(6), 973–996.

Lang, D., Wiek, A., Bergmann, M., Stauffacher, M., Martens, P., Moll, P., Swilling, M., & Thomas, C. (2012). Transdisciplinary research in sustainability science: Practice, principles, and challenges. *Sustainability Science, 7*(Suppl 1), 25–43.

Leonard, D., Becker, R., & Coate, K. (2005). To prove myself at the highest level: The benefits of doctoral study. *Higher Education Research & Development, 24*(2), 135–149.

Lomas, J. (1997, November). *Improving research dissemination and uptake in the health sector: Beyond the sound of one hand clapping* (Policy Commentary C97-1). Hamilton: McMaster University Centre for Health Economics and Policy Analysis.

Loxley, A., & Seery, A. (2008). Some philosophical and other related issues of insider research. In P. Sikes & A. Potts (Eds.), *Researching education rom the inside: Investigations from within* (pp. 15–32). London: Routledge.

Loxley, A., & Seery, A. (2012). The role of the professional doctorate in Ireland from the student perspective. *Studies in Higher Education, 37*(1), 3–17.

Lucas, P. (2012 October 29–November 2). *Critical reflection: What do we really mean?* (pp. 163–167). Proceedings of the Australian Collaborative Education Network (ACEN) National Conference, Deakin University, Geelong, Australia.

McCay, G. (2010). *Taught professional doctorates: An overview of structure, content and their role within the professional community.* University of Edinburgh, Scotland. Retrieved February 15, 2016, from http://www.docs.sasg.ed.ac.uk/AcademicServices/Staff/Curriculum/What_is_a_professional_doctorate.pdf

Mellors-Bourne, R., Robinson, C., & Metcalfe, J. (2016). *Provision of professional doctorates in English HE institutions.* Cambridge: Careers Research & Advisory Centre (CRAC) Ltd.

Mercer, J. (2007). The challenges of insider research in educational institutions: Wielding a double-edged sword and resolving delicate dilemmas. *Oxford Review of Education, 33*(1), 1–17.

Miller, P., Moore, D., & Strang, J. (2006). The regulation of research by funding bodies: An emerging ethical issue for the alcohol and other drug sector? *International Journal of Drug Policy, 17*(1), 12–16.

Morris, M., Leung, K., Ames, D., & Lickel, B. (1999). Views from the inside and outside: Integrating emic and etic insights about culture and justice judgement. *Academy of Management Review, 24*(4), 781–796.

Mullings, B. (1999). Insider or outsider, both or neither: Some dilemmas of interviewing in a cross-cultural setting. *Geoforum, 30*, 337–350.

Noffke, S. (1997). Professional, personal, and political dimensions of action research. *Review of Research in Education, 22*, 305–343.

Pillow, W. (2010). Dangerous reflexivity: Rigour, responsibility and reflexivity in qualitative research. In P. Thomson & M. Walker (Eds.), *The Routledge doctoral students' companion* (pp. 270–282). London: Routledge.

Rearick, M., & Feldman, A. (1999). Orientations, purposes and reflection: A framework for understanding action research. *Teaching and Teacher Education, 15*, 333–349.

Reed, J., & Procter, S. (1995). *Practitioner research in health care: The inside story.* London: Chapman and Hall.

Rossman, G., & Rallis, S. (2012). *Learning in the field: An introduction to qualitative research* (3rd ed.). Thousand Oaks, CA: Sage.

Scott, D., Brown, A., Lunt, I., & Thorne, L. (2004). *Professional doctorates: Integrating professional and academic knowledge*. Buckingham: Society for Research into Higher Education / Open University Press.

Shenton, A. (2004). Strategies for ensuring trustworthiness in qualitative research projects. *Education for Information, 22*, 63–75.

Sikes, P., & Potts, A. (Eds.). (2008). *Researching education from the inside: Investigations from within*. London: Routledge.

Smyth, A., & Holian, R. (2008). Credibility issues in research from within organisations. In P. Sikes & A. Potts (Eds.), *Researching education from the inside: Investigations from within* (pp. 33–47). London: Routledge.

Spradley, J. (1980). *Participant observation*. New York, NY: Holt, Rinehart and Winston.

Taylor, A. (2007). Learning to become a researching professional: The case of the Doctorate of Education. *International Journal of Teaching and Learning in Higher Education, 19*(2), 154–166.

Wenger, E. (1998). *Communities of practice: Learning, meaning and identity*. Cambridge: Cambridge University Press.

Wildy, H., Peden, S., & Chan, K. (2014). The rise of professional doctorates: Case studies of the Doctorate in Education in China, Iceland and Australia. *Studies in Higher Education, 40*(5), 761–774.

Williams, K. (2010). 'Guilty knowledge': The (im)possibility of ethical security in social science research. In P. Thomson & M. Walker (Eds.), *The Routledge doctoral students' companion* (pp. 256–269). London: Routledge.

Wind, G. (2008). Negotiated interactive observation: Doing fieldwork in hospital settings. *Anthropology & Medicine, 15*(2), 79–89.

PART 2

THEORISING DOCTORATE JOURNEYING

TATJANA DRAGOVIC

5. THE ART AND CRAFT OF PROFESSIONAL DOCTORATES

INTRODUCTION

I saw the angel in the marble and carved until I set him free. (Michelangelo)

When I stood for the first time in front of a clean canvas feeling an uplifting and uncontrollable urge to paint my vision, I felt inspired, passionate and driven. At the same time I knew that for that vision to be transferred into paint brush strokes and into the explosion of vibrant colours I saw and felt inside of me, I needed to know how to use different painting techniques and acquire the accompanying sets of skills in order to achieve the effect I envisaged. And yet I started painting as I could not wait for all the techniques and skills to be acquired first. I feared missing the right moment for capturing the vision in its freshness, relevance and opulence. So I learned the craft on the way, with and from artists/painters/experts, and kept integrating all the techniques and skills and on that complex journey of simultaneously learning 'how to' and creating 'what' I intrinsically felt urged to express through my painting, there were elements of struggle, painful setbacks, confusion and despair. But there were also elements of joy, transformation, passion, and hope. Through this multi-layered and overlapping journey my creation had changed, developed and yielded an even greater, more colourful, more vibrant and more powerful effect than expected, and I had become a different person who arrived at a place that was unknown to me and yet I felt at home. It was time to set my creation free, to step back and let it flow into its own course of life.

Twelve years ago I felt a similar uplifting and uncontrollable urge to paint my vision for professional teacher education practice. I knew 'what' was driving me, I knew 'what' I wanted to improve, and I knew that I wanted to continue working as a teacher educator while studying the practice. It is little wonder that a professional doctorate in education with its focus on researching my own practice while still working was my first and only choice. Yet, even though I knew 'what' I wanted to research, I still had to learn 'how to' do it, not in terms of acquiring the craft of researchers, but rather in terms of balancing with one foot in professional practice and the other in the academic world, while juggling family commitments and newly acquired parenthood. Five years ago I felt a similar urge to teach and supervise professional doctorate students, to be a companion on their journeys and to witness their transformations. I knew 'what' I wanted to do and had to learn 'how to' do it.

Not in terms of how to teach professional doctorate students, but rather in terms of being there for them, being curious about their practice and above all 'holding the space' for them to feel both safe and challenged.

This introductory chapter to Part 2 'Theorising doctorate journeying practices for professionals' will firstly focus on the 'what' and 'how' of 'doing' a professional doctorate and supervising/teaching professional doctorate students in order to explore 'crafting mastery' behind transformative journeys. Craft is usually defined as skill in planning, making or executing, and professional doctorate students certainly need skills and techniques to plan their long doctoral journeys alongside their professional and personal journeys. The chapter will then embark on exploring the 'artistic' elements of doing a professional doctorate, the ones that cannot be meticulously planned and executed and yet they leave a distinct transformative trace. Art can be seen and understood as human endowment (Dissanayake, 1988) and as a creative process producing works to be appreciated primarily for their beauty or emotional power. During their professional doctorate, students frequently discover that their final product (portfolio or dissertation) is far from being the only creation of their journey. They find the creation of their new professional identity (that of a researching professional) equally, if not more, emotionally powerful. At the end of the chapter and of 'the hero's journey' (Campbell, 1949) artistic elements and crafting mastery of professional doctorates will be 'reunited' demonstrating how challenges and temptations on the way contribute to the 'hero's' transformation and to the journey from the 'ordinary/known/everyday world' to the 'unknown' one, i.e. from the known world of practitioners to the unknown world of researching professionals.

THE CRAFT OF PROFESSIONAL DOCTORATES

This Is Water

> There are two young fish swimming along and they happen to meet an older fish swimming the other way, who nods at them and says "*Morning, boys. How's the water?*" And the two young fish swim on for a bit, and then eventually one of them looks over at the other and asks "*What is water?*" Wallace (2009)

The known world of professional practice has its great strength in being exactly that – known and familiar. However, what is familiar is sometimes not understood or known precisely because it is familiar. The fish story mentioned above expresses exactly that point. Most practitioners embarking on a professional doctorate are very familiar with their practice and its potential strengths and flaws, and yet they get surprised when their professional doctorate route brings them unexpected discoveries about their own practice. In the chapters that follow our students discuss their journeys with all the unintended and unexpected surprises on the way. What makes practitioners choose a professional doctorate and what is it they are hoping to achieve?

Crayer (2000) makes a distinction between 'essential' and 'supporting' reasons for undertaking a research degree. Although many authors and postgraduate students may disagree with her classification (e.g. career advancement is defined as a supporting reason) one needs to acknowledge the impact her classification has on stimulating the reflective process about one's own reasons for doing postgraduate research. In his discussion of Crayer, Potter (2006) lists his own table of five essential reasons for undertaking a research degree:

1. Personal development,
2. To be able to make a difference – for example, a desire to change practice in work or to learn more about a 'condition' that a student or members of their family have experienced,
3. To follow a new or better career,
4. Burning interest in a topic (intellectual curiosity),
5. To keep one's mind active (p. 23).

The above list can be equally valid for both professional doctorate students and for other doctoral students, except that the second reason (a desire to change practice) resonates more with professional doctorates. The urge that was described above as a drive for artistic endeavour can be found in the wish to be able to make a difference in one's own practice. Scott et al. (2004) refer to three main reasons for embarking on a professional doctorate journey: extrinsic-professional initiation, extrinsic-professional continuation and intrinsic-personal/professional affirmation. What seems to be common to Potter and Scott et al. is that personal/professional development is both expected and desired, and a burning wish to research and improve one's own practice is present. I can recognize both in myself as my personal experience of being a teacher in the midst of the Balkan civil wars contributed to a burning wish to research the field of development and sustainability of teachers' professional identity in order for me to be able to personally and professionally develop, and above all to make a difference within the teaching of professional practice (my water). So can a professional doctorate help us research our own 'water' in spite of our deep situatedness that can prevent us from seeing the obvious like in the fish story?

A Hero's Journey

The craft part of professional doctorates starts with that call to awaken (and to finally recognize the 'water') and begin the journey. Campbell's (1949) definition of a hero is related to his modern interpretation of mythic themes. It is a metaphor well suited for our professional doctorate students. Campbell argues that myths carry the human spirit forward and describes a typical pattern of a hero's journey as full of hurdles. The professional doctorate students contributing to this book shared their narratives of how their spirits were carried forward in spite of all the challenges on the way. The hero's journey as analysed by Campbell has several well-defined and set phases.

The journey begins with the departure, which includes the call to awaken and very often the hero tries to resist the call before s/he embraces it completely. As a former professional doctorate student I remember my self-doubt about whether I can afford to pursue my call, not only at the beginning of the professional doctorate journey but also in later phases when not all colleagues were supportive and understanding. As a doctoral educator and a supervisor I came to understand and appreciate professional doctorate students' commitment when after a long day at work they drive for two to three hours to come to a lecture or a supervisory meeting. Moran (2009) found, while examining the role commitment played in the careers of 36 professionals, that commitment can play different roles. She distinguished between those for whom commitment compensates (keeps them going), 'experimentalists' for whom commitment defies and 'domain transformers' for whom commitment impassions. It could be interesting to carry out a similar examination of the role of commitment on professional doctorate students and explore how many would be defined as 'domain transformers'. There does not seem to be any doubt that commitment is a key element in professional doctorate students' lives, as they balance their private, professional and academic lives and slowly move from their everyday world into new uncharted territory (Figure 1). Thus their first set of skills belonging to the crafting mastery of maintaining professional doctorate journey is handling *commitment* in spite of hurdles and challenges; taking the paint brushes and starting to paint committedly from the very first moment of experiencing that inspirational urge/drive. Doctoral educators and supervisors would need to understand that not each and every brushstroke would be perfect but rather experimental and above all committed – something to acknowledge and encourage in order to contribute to the sustainability of the long and demanding journey. Professional doctorate students cannot wait to first acquire all the necessary skills before they start painting, (i.e. researching their own practice) as there is almost an urgency and immediacy in wanting to make a difference now and not in a few years and to transfer a burning wish into action and desired changes.

In my doctoral education and supervisory practice I used and tested coaching as a tool for supporting changes that my professional doctorate students set out to introduce and implement. Although there are variations across different coaching programmes, the common theme of coaching is that it is facilitative rather than instructional (Creasy & Patterson, 2005) with the process resting on the coach reflecting back to the learner what they observe or hear, in order to help the learner set goals, resolve problems and take action. This coaching approach draws from Whitmore's (2002) GROW model (goal, reality, option, will) where reflection can lead to change in practice. The International Coach Federation, the oldest professional body in the coaching field, defines coaching as 'an on-going interactive relationship that helps individuals (and/or groups and organizations) deepen their learning and initiate new patterns of thinking in order to achieve extraordinary results" [*on line*]. As the coaching approach assumes that the person who is coached has all the potentials to achieve the change they desire, doctoral educators and supervisors might explore a possibility of developing a set of coaching skills that includes asking powerful questions, giving constructive feedback, future-orientation and 'not knowing' as a principle of avoiding 'spoon-feeding' students theories and models, but rather supporting them in their own exploration of useful models for their study/ies. A specific set of coaching skills for doctoral educators and supervisors could be, for this initial phase, to employ genuine *curiosity*, when professional doctorate students made those first 'paint brush strokes' with 'an unsteady hand' but with burning interest.

HERO'S JOURNEY

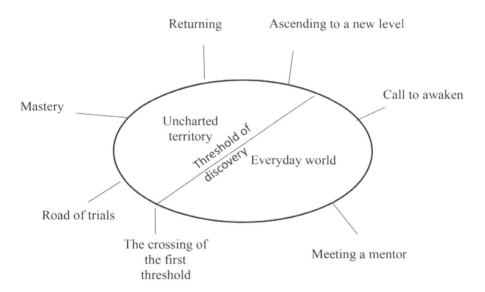

Figure 1. Hero's journey (adapted from Campbell, 1949)

According to Campbell, after the call and initial doubts, the hero meets a helper/ mentor who supports and provides him/her with tools to proceed. The role of a doctoral educator and supervisor as a helper/mentor in this early phase of a hero's journey i.e. early stage of a professional doctorate is pivotal as the next phase encompasses the crossing of the first threshold meaning leaving behind the previous life and entering a new one. The tools the student's helper/mentor/supervisor/doctoral educator provides include a set of researcher's skills necessary for carrying out a practice-based study/ies. The students will need these tools as leaving behind the pure professional world and entering the intertwined world of practice and academic realms of experience requires a crafting mastery to handle the shift. Vulnerability and critical awareness that accompanies the shift from the old to the new world surprised me in my role of a professional doctorate student and taught me to be a sympathetic and considerate doctoral educator and supervisor. The reader may keep in mind that my account has been created after the event and many authors have demonstrated how such accounts may contain 'fictive elements' e.g. Clements (1999) refers to the 'fictive voice' in autobiographical research by which the teller, through critique, may 'arrive at an accurate recreation of one's professional past' (1999, p. 21). However, some of the professional doctorate students/contributors to the book are currently experiencing the phase of crossing the first threshold and their poignant stories clearly illustrate their vulnerability. Thus the second set of crafting skills for professional doctorate students encompasses, besides research skills, the openness to one's own *vulnerability* when making a shift from own 'water' to new uncharted 'waters'. When students experience their own vulnerability, the intimate process they are going through can be carefully and tactfully supported by the silent and yet strong (physical or virtual i.e. via emails or phones) *presence* and by the availability of a 'helper'/doctoral educator and supervisor.

The transition into the new world is not always smooth, as the hero is met by a gatekeeper s/he needs to negotiate with in order to enter fully the new world, and many professional doctorate students refer to their interim summative assessment as hurdles they need to overcome. Once the hero is inside the new world – the combined world of practice and research – s/he is in the phase of initiation surrounded both by 'enemies' and 'aids'. For professional doctorate students lots of craft, skills and competencies are needed to not only continue carrying out their research, but also to negotiate trials on the way that can come in the form of sudden changes in the professional setting or family context. This is where craft becomes obviously needed both on the side of the professional doctorate student, who is challenged to use *reflexivity* and *critical awareness* of their own situation, and on the side of the doctoral educators and supervisors to facilitate the student's *resilience* with carefully chosen strategies. Peers can be a great source of support and of opportunities to model successful strategies. It is in this phase of initiation that professional doctorate students experience personal transformation, growth and illumination. For that process they need another set of skills i.e. *reflexivity, critical awareness and negotiation skills* to be used with the representatives of both worlds (professional and academic) and above all with their own reflexive self. Doctoral educators and supervisors may explore the idea of using carefully designed *stretching questions* that simultaneously support and stretch their students' reflexivity beyond current challenges to the future effects of the current setbacks on their growth and personal transformation.

The hero's journey moves to closure with the crossing of the second threshold when s/he becomes a master of both worlds, experiences great discoveries and returns as a different person to the world s/he left in order to share what s/he has learned and ascend to a new level. The following chapters are professional doctorate students' narratives of their hero's transformative journeys. In their concluding reflections they share with the readers that the writing process itself was contributing to their personal/professional development. Goodall's comment that "in writing, as in speaking, we come to *know*" (2000, p. 127) is clearly supported by the students' accounts. For this phase of dissemination of their learning, professional doctorate students need *communication* skills both for *writing and presenting practices.* As a doctoral educator and supervisor I encourage professional doctorate students to document their journey and the shifts between the two worlds (professional and academic). A simple tool also used in coaching is for doctoral supervisors to catalyst their students' efforts by providing *constructive feedback* that focuses on what is well phrased and what could be improved.

As both professional doctorate students and their educators/supervisors develop crafting mastery for their journeys, there is still a range of artistic elements that cannot be planned, timed or even executed according to anybody's wishes or interests but do leave an unforgettable transformative trace. The subtle (or sometimes abrupt) shifts in their professional identities are part of the creative/artistic processes, those which produce 'works' i.e. changes to be appreciated for their emotional power – these changes and how to support them through artistic processes are discussed in the next section.

THE ART OF PROFESSIONAL DOCTORATES

In the preface of the book Pam Burnard explores the intertwining identity of the researching professional as being co-created by the identity of practitioners who 'do it' (being situated in professional practices) and the identity of researchers/scholars who 'study it' (being situated in the academic practice). Beijaard et al. (2004) emphasized that professional identity implies both person (the professional) and context (the professional practice) – both of which are changing and co-influencing each other. Professional doctorate students start their journey as accomplished and experienced practitioners and need to acquire skills to negotiate all the trials and navigate through their 'hero's journey'. The creative process of moving from being a knowledgeable practitioner to the place of 'not knowing' can be both exciting and painful. In spite of the skills professional doctorate students may use (handling commitment, being open to their own vulnerability, being reflexive, etc.), managing the shift from the identity of a knowledgeable practitioner to a researching professional, which would encompass both 'the doing' part of a practitioner and 'the studying part' of a researcher/scholar, is a demanding task. It is an artistic task as it is human endowment and a process that produces work to be appreciated for its emotional power. This new professional identity is bigger than the sum of the two parts that it encompasses, and as Strauss (1962) argues, it can become a model of personal change or development that would challenge the 'substantial self' laid down in the multitude of interactions in the past. In his discussion of transformations of identity and self, one meets with new concepts and new classifications, as old ones are being modified. Transformations involve "radical change of action and person" since they "connote shifts in perceiving, remembering and valuing" (p. 66). They necessitate "new evolutions: of self and others, of events, acts and objects;

and the transformation of perception is irreversible; once having changed, there is no going back" (ibid.). Wenger introduces the idea of professional identity as being forged within the context of the profession, but that it transcends its boundaries by saying that 'the experience of identity in practice is a way of being in the world" (Wenger, 1998, p. 151).

Professional doctorate students thus do not just make a shift from 'the doing' practitioner (who 'paints' committedly within his own practice) to 'the studying' researcher (who examines and analyses the painting), but create artistically a new professional identity that not only encompasses the previous two, but transcends them into, as Wenger suggests, 'the being in the world' (Figure 2).

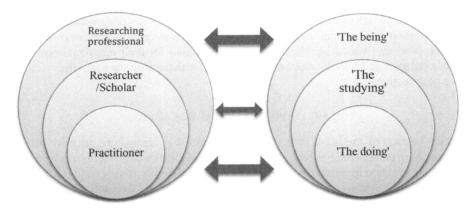

Figure 2. Overarching identity of the researching professional

This artistic process of co-constructing a new identity needs to be supported both by professional doctorate students themselves and by doctoral educators and supervisors (ideally also by peers in both the professional and the academic world and by friends and families). Just as professional doctorate students experience a merging of the practitioner and researcher identity into a researching professional one, doctoral educators and supervisors may experience their own identity transformation from being doctoral supervisors to being professional doctorate supervisors who are taking into account all the shades of the newly created identity of their students and matching them accordingly.

Dissanayake (1988) takes an interesting ethological or bioevolutionary approach to art and characterizes it as a behaviour. She provocatively asks "why did a behavior of art arise at all" and "what does art contribute to human species that would account for its appearance in the human repertoire?" (p. 6). One of the reasons, as established earlier, for professional doctorate students to start their journey is rooted in their wish to develop, improve and contribute to their own professional practice, to create something that is of a particular value. So does the behaviour of wanting to create a change, make a difference in their own practice belong to the professional doctorate students' repertoire, and if yes, could it be considered artistic?

Preminger's (2012) review of the transformative nature of art uses the neurobiological approach and claims that on-going experience of arts and of artistic processes may alter cognitive, emotional, and behavioral patterns as well as their underlying neural circuits. Csikszentmihalyi (1990) researched extensively artists (and sportsmen) and defined their state of flow as a state of deep absorption and immersion in an intrinsically enjoyable activity. Maslow (1968) explored a similar state (referring to it as 'peak experience') when feeling happy. As doctoral educators and supervisors whenever we spent at least half an hour with a professional doctorate student and prompted him/her to share his research interest, we would experience the student's 'flow' as s/he shares enthusiastically details about their research and professional practice. Csikszentmihalyi illustrates the idea in a diagram as a matter of balancing skills (craft) and challenge (unplanned and unpredictable part of a journey), where flow is achieved when there is a high level of both skills and challenge and they are in balance (Figure 3). In line with Preminger's idea that on-going experience of art or artistic processes may bring about transformations along with changes in cognitive, emotional and behavioural patterns, the question arises: "How could the naturally occurring flow (which we witnessed in doctoral and supervisory sessions when professional doctorate students were encouraged to talk about their practice-based research) be initiated more frequently and sustained over the whole length of a doctoral journey?"

According to Csikszentmihalyi it is easy to achieve flow if we are aware (self-reflection) of what we need in order to feel skilful/capable and what we need to feel appropriately challenged. Professional doctorate students might want to explore how to reflect on the two elements of the graph while doctoral educators and supervisors might purposefully provide conditions and or activities for their students to feel first capable and then gradually challenged. As a consequence, doctoral educators and supervisors may also experience a state of deep immersion and absorbtion in the activity itself and thus join their students in the state of flow.

Writing practices seem to be one of the fields where professional doctorate students may use more artistic and flow elements in order to achieve not only their own state of flow, but also the flow of their written accounts. All our students (without any exception) who contributed chapters to the book talked to us and wrote about the transformative effect the writing for the chapters had on them. Many of them timidly shared that in the past they experienced 'artist's block' when ideas seemed to disappear. By talking about artist's block, professional doctorate students clearly situate themselves as 'artists' or as creators of written accounts that might have, as described earlier, emotional power. Doctoral educators and supervisors could contribute to more effective writing practices by creating first 'low stake' opportunities for students to write in a free flow manner during the sessions followed by analysis and a next round of writing on a higher level. Thus professional doctorate students could experience both artistic writing processes and a state of flow while being immersed in writing.

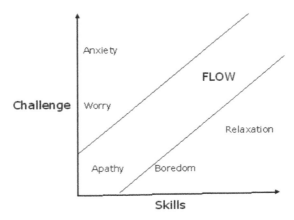

Figure 3. Flow according to Csikszentmihalyi (1990)

THE ART AND CRAFT OF PROFESSIONAL DOCTORATES

The three bricklayers were working side by side when somebody comes along and asked each of them, "*What are you doing?*" The first bricklayer replies, "*I'm laying bricks.*" The second bricklayer replies, "*I'm building a wall.*" The third says: "*I'm building a cathedral.*"

Professional doctorate students no doubt need to master the craft of carrying out their research as well as the craft of balancing multiple journeys while shifting their professional identity from being a practitioner to being a researching professional. They need to know how to lay bricks. However, without being inspired and driven to see the bigger picture, to focus on the cathedral they might miss the opportunity to capture their visions of better professional practices. The right combination of crafting mastery and an inspirational artistic approach may be a way forward for new generations of researching professionals bridging the realms of practice and theory. The overview of the crafting and artistic elements below (Table 1) might be used as a reminder of the complexity of the researching professional/hero's journey and of the support needed for a passage from the 'ordinary/known/everyday world' to the 'unknown' one, i.e. from the known world of practitioners to the unknown world of researching professionals.

With the careful and on-going use of skills for maintaining commitment, being open to vulnerability, developing resilience and good written and oral presentations skills, professional doctorate students might be well equipped to confidently experience merging old and new identities and through flow become researching professionals.

Doctoral supervisors and educators could contribute to their students' hero's journeys by showing genuine curiosity, maintaining (literal or virtual) presence and availability, asking stretching questions and providing constructive feedback. Hopefully, by accompanying their students, doctoral supervisors and educators will develop a new identity as well.

Table 1. Overview of the art and craft of professional doctorates as exemplified in students' and doctoral educators'/supervisors' practices

	THE ART and CRAFT of PROFESSIONAL DOCTORATES	
	Doctoral students	*Doctoral educators and supervisors*
CRAFT	Maintaining commitment	Showing genuine curiosity through asking questions
	Openness to and handling of vulnerability	Maintaining (literal or virtual) presence and availability
	Developing resilience through reflexivity, critical awareness and negotiation skills	Asking stretching questions
	Developing communication skills (writing and presenting practices)	Providing constructive feedback
ART	Experiencing merging identities from 'the doing' to 'the studying' to 'the being'	Experiencing merging identities from being doctoral supervisor to being a professional doctorate supervisor
	Experiencing flow	Experiencing flow

CONCLUDING COMMENTS

A great work is never finished, it is just abandoned. (Picasso)

Here I am, 'abandoning' the chapter and setting it free to flow into its own course of life and leaving the readers to experience and explore the chapters in Part 2 that aim to capture the art and craft of professional doctorate journeys as experienced by students. While theorizing their practices professional doctorate students are sharing a transformative journey from practitioners to researching professionals thus creating a new professional identity and in writing about their practices 'translating' them into academic texts. Gavin Turner (Chapter 6) is sharing his tentative early steps towards a shift in the mindset from being a practitioner to becoming a researching professional; James Knowles (Chapter 7), in a true story of a hero's journey, illustrates how setbacks and challenges can lead to a marvellous transformation and Denise Whalley (Chapter 8) unwraps the power of vulnerability by taking us through a poignant but fascinating shift in her professional identity.

With the hope that the following chapters will take the readers on their own journeys exploring the development of their own professional identities over time, whether affected by embarking on a professional doctorate study, supervision or any other, professionally (and personally) transformative journey, I move to another 'canvas' enriched and transformed by the experience of supporting, and editing students' accounts and collaborating with inspirational colleagues.

REFERENCES

Beijaard, D., Meijer, P. C., & Verloop, N. (2004). Reconsidering research on teachers' professional identity. *Teacher and Teaching Education, 20*, 107–128.

Campbell, J. (1949). *The hero with a thousand faces.* Princeton, NJ: Princeton University Press.

Crayer, P. (2000). *The research student's guide to success.* Buckingham: Open University Press.

Creasy, J., & Patterson, F. (2005). *Leading personalised learning.* Nottingham: National College for Teaching and Leadership (NCTL).

Clements, P. (1999). Autobiographical research and the emergence of the fictive voice. *Cambridge Journal of Education, 29*(1), 21–32.

Csikszentmihalyi, M. (1990). *Flow: The psychology of optimal experience*: New York, NY: Harper.

Dissanayake, E. (1988). *What is art for?* Seattle, WA: University of Washington Press.

Goodall, H. L. (2000). *Writing the new ethnography.* New York, NY: Altamira Press.

International Coach Federation. (n.d). Retrieved March 1, 2005, from http://www.coachfederation.org

Maslow, A. (1968). *Toward a psychology of being.* Hoboken, NJ: John Wiley & Sons.

Moran, S. (2009). What role does commitment play among writers with different levels of creativity? *Creativity Research Journal, 21*(2&3), 243–257.

Potter, S. (2006). *Doing postgraduate research.* London: Sage Publications.

Preminger, S. (2012). Transformative art: Art as means for long-term neurocognitive change. *Frontiers in Human Neuroscience, 6*(96), 1–7. doi:10.3389/fnhum.2012.00096

Scott, D., Brown, A., Lunt, I. & Thorne, L. (2004). *Professional doctorates: Integrating professional and academic knowledge.* Maidenhead: Open University Press.

Strauss, A. (1962). Transformations of identity. In A. M. Rose (Ed.), *Human behaviour and social processes.* London: Routledge & Kegan Paul.

Wallace, D. F. (2009). *This is water* (pp. 3–4). New York, NY: Little, Brown and Company.

Wenger, E. (1998). *Communities of practice: Learning, meaning and identity.* Cambridge: Cambridge University Press.

Whitmore, J. (2002). *Coaching for performance.* London: Nicholas Brealey.

GAVIN TURNER

6. THE TEACHER AS A LEARNER

Theorising a Shift in Mindset at the Start of My
Professional Doctorate Journey

INTRODUCTION

This chapter presents a reflexive and theoretically framed account of the fundamental shift in mindset that I experienced during my first term as a Doctorate of Education (EdD) student – a movement away from a purely practice-based professional focus towards displaying the habits and dispositions of a researching professional. It outlines the experiences that have encouraged this change in mindset, as well as examining a wide range of literature to support theoretical discussion of how and why this movement has occurred. This shift has been facilitated by the challenge of engaging with doctoral research at one of the most famous universities in the world, leading to the perceived pressure of creating new and substantive knowledge alongside the desire to generate a profound impact on both my own practice and that of others. Would I be capable of achieving this? Would I be able to hold my own amongst such heavyweight academics? Would I be able to maintain my motivation to learn over the five years of part-time study, despite unforeseen changes in my professional and personal life? Could I offer insights into many unforeseen and unforeseeable instantiations where I see the practical, academic and affective changes at work that have both encouraged and resulted from the shift in mindset since embarking on my professional doctorate journey?

Since this chapter focuses on the change and transformation of my mindset over the course of my first term of doctoral study, it is important to define the term 'mindset' in terms of how it will be used in this chapter. I would like to define mindset as the set of beliefs and attitudes that you hold for yourself. Fang et al. (2004, p. 298) describe the mindset as something that "occurs in a person's head", giving rise to the potential for one's mindset to influence or control personal behaviour. The link between mindset and behaviour is central to this chapter, as it outlines how internally held attitudes and beliefs about myself have fundamentally shifted "from one way of thinking to another", giving rise to changes in my behaviour that increasingly reflect the dispositions of a researching practitioner (Fang et al., 2004, p. 298). These thoughts emphasise the importance of external, socio-cultural stimuli on the beliefs and attitudes that form my mindset, but additionally how my mindset is influenced by a constantly changing and diverse range of professional and learning experiences,

P. Burnard et al. (Eds.), Transformative Doctoral Research Practices for Professionals, 75–89.

highlighting the dynamic and malleable nature of the mindset rather than being a fixed, solely internal, entity.

Working as professionals in education sectors, Andrews and Edwards (2008, p. 4) who both followed the Doctor of Education (EdD) rather than the Doctor of Philosophy pathway, write that: "It was tempting at first to think of oneself as a deficit model, but gradually we began to move forward with more confidence". This perspective accurately describes my own thoughts as I stood at the grand gates of professional doctoral research, ready to take my first tentative steps on my EdD journey. A deficit model is characterised by weak understanding resulting from a lack of information, something that I can certainly recognise in myself as I arrived at the faculty for the induction and first lectures. Walford (1991, p. 2) refers to how the "novice researcher" will see difficulties and ambiguities as a personal deficiency arising from insufficient knowledge and the process of emergence before doctoral experiences erupt on their professional scene. This may be because of the role of expertise and mastery in professional practice and forms of institutional performance indicators operating at national and international levels. Walford's thoughts validate the efficacious doubts and feelings that I was experiencing during these opening exchanges and, despite research experience at Masters level where small-scale research and professional practice were successfully combined, it was with faltering confidence and nervous excitement that I began my EdD journey with a lecture delivered by one of the editors of this book, Tatjana Dragovic, titled "Becoming a Researching Professional". This lecture acted as a catalyst for the shift in mindset from a purely practice-focused outlook, stimulating thought on what it means to be a research practitioner with a foot in both camps; a position of which I have only limited experience and understanding. This shift was, in part, fostered and encouraged by the interaction with my peer group, fellow first-year professional doctorate students. I was struck by both the richness and depth of discussion, even at this early stage in our learning journey, giving rise to my reflection on the importance of collaboration in the construction of new knowledge. Somekh (1994) examines collaboration by making effective use of Bruner's (1986) metaphor of inhabiting each other's castles. She states that through collaboration, contributing and learning become a single process, allowing me to develop knowledge and understanding of other's castles where movement between them "is pleasurable, challenging and mutually empowering" (Somekh, 1994, p. 373). Like both Andrews and Edwards, my confidence began to grow and I, along with my fellow doctoral students, made progress through the opening stages of our five-year journey.

I have always been an ambitious and aspirational individual, traits which drove me to submit my application to join the Doctor of Education pathway. However, when thinking practically, a major source of conflict is potentially the demands on my time between my professional practice and my research goals; a tension which will inevitably heighten as I progress through the five years of part-time study. Palmer (2007, p. 83) describes the contention of successful teaching as "holding the tension of opposites". This is a metaphor that resonates strongly with me, as the nervous excitement felt on arriving at the faculty for the first time since interview represents a clear and palpable 'tension' in emotion. However, looking beyond this early tension it is clear to me that if I am to successfully navigate my way across the vast expanse of the EdD ocean, I will need to manage the temporal conflict and, as Palmer states, hold the "tension of opposites" within my control. Moreover, this conflict extends beyond the purely practical, encompassing further tensions between research and profession, theory and practice, teacher and learner. Morrissey (2014, p. 841) develops Palmer's dichotomy by suggesting how, as a teacher, she has been 'trained' to separate the tensions that exist between the personal and professional, body and mind, teacher and learner. I perceive that the separation created by these tensions of opposites will result in the polarisation and, in turn, potential weakening of both facets of my stance as a researching practitioner; professional practice and research. Instead, however, I believe I need to 'untrain' my default mindset and re-tune it to draw on the strengths of both. Despite my strong roots and experience as a teaching practitioner, can I re-tune my mindset to successfully combine practice and research goals?

THE TEACHER AS A RESEARCHER

As I continue to consider the context, design and theoretical underpinnings of my research focus during the opening stages of the course, it is imperative that I become able to position myself within the research-practice nexus. As with all real world settings, my professional context has its own unique blend of challenges and idiosyncrasies and I would argue that the context-specific nature of the setting requires a tailored and bespoke approach to educational improvement. This argument forms the basis for the case of engaging in educational research as a researching practitioner, as I am not only able to observe the opportunities for improvement within the setting, but I am also able to play an active role in the development, implementation and evaluation of pedagogical interventions with a view to offering an enhanced learning environment for the learners that I teach. It is this belief, perhaps above all else, that motivated me to challenge my own professional development by applying to engage in doctoral study.

Whilst considering professional development it is interesting to express the encouragement and support provided by the senior leaders within my school, making me feel empowered to investigate what actually happens in the classroom, with a vision of challenging and changing it when pedagogically necessary. When I look back on my own professional journey from initial teacher training to now, it is clear that my practice has been increasingly influenced by experience and internal professional development processes rather than engagement with educational theory. Despite the imbalance between professional practice and educational research experience, I would argue that my ten years of classroom experience places me in a position to challenge and change pedagogical strategies through educational research, as I have considerable experience of observing and measuring the learning outcomes which are a direct response to my own practice and, as such, I am well-placed to identify deficiencies in practice and target specific areas for development. As a classroom practitioner I am driven by the constant desire to improve my own practice as a professional and I believe that the acquisition of the habits and dispositions of a researcher through engagement with the EdD professional doctorate opens up new pathways. These journeys prioritise knowledge creation through its capacity to entwine professional experience and expertise with scholarly discourse, theory use and theory building and will not only support pedagogical progress, but have the potential to enhance my own practice to levels far beyond that achieved solely through context-specific professional development.

Praxis Makes Perfect

Hammersley (2004, p. 167), assesses the difference in status between *praxis* (action) and *theoria* (research). This difference is founded in an influential strand of Classical Greek philosophy that regarded *praxis* and *theoria* as different ways of life, and, moreover, as ways of life occupying different hierarchical status. These two opposing positions are further defined, as *theoria* involves detachment from, and *praxis* immersion in, the events that make up human social life (Hammersley, 2004, p. 167). Hammersley (2004, p. 168) suggests that, based on this hierarchy, to conflate these two ideas is not just to combine two conflicting ideologies, but also works to "betray the higher nature of *theoria*". This conflation of two opposing positions links strongly to Palmer's "tension of opposites" discussed earlier in the chapter; it is this tension of opposites that I am experiencing as I attempt to retune my mindset from teacher to learner and from practitioner to researching practitioner. However, I contest the view that it is a betrayal of the higher nature. I would argue that by uniting the two ideologies, just as I am doing as a researching practitioner, provides the strongest position from which to conduct educational research; by engaging with the critical evaluation of both positions and drawing on the ideological strengths of each, it provides a very strong framework through which I can research and try to improve the educational setting in which I practice.

The combination of these ancient and contrasting standpoints leads me into more modern times and to reflect on Stenhouse's (1975) revival of early notions of action research, where he considers the concept of the "teacher as researcher". Stenhouse argued for practitioners to undertake research themselves to improve educational practice. Stenhouse (1975, p. 205) states, "it is the teachers who in the end will change the world of the school by understanding it". I strongly believe that the teacher-as-researcher's position of being immersed in practice is a position of strength as it allows for the subjective identification of practical problems whilst retaining some sense of objectivity provided through the methodological and ethical considerations relevant to research. By acquiring an enhanced understanding of the context-specific problems through educational research I, as a researching practitioner, am able to "change the world of the school", or certainly my own place within it. Hammersley's thoughts support this belief. Hammersley states that "the core idea of action research is that there should be an intimate relationship between inquiry and practical or political activities – such that the focus of inquiry arises out of, and its results feed back into, the activity concerned" (2004, p. 165). In further support of this perspective, McKernan (1996, p. 4) states, "action research is carried out by practitioners seeking to improve their understanding of events, situations and problems so as to increase the effectiveness of their practice". It is also important to note McKernan's use of the word 'effectiveness' when discussing the role of action research in the development of practice. As a conscientious and mindful practitioner I am constantly trying to enhance the effectiveness of my practice to provide a more powerful learning environment; however, I believe that the role of action research goes beyond this distinct goal and aligns with one of the EdD's underpinning ideals – *impact* on practice. The impact of doctoral study is often conceptualised as the outcomes and benefits of research; however, impact is operationally defined as "an effect that is a consequence or result of a particular process event, action or phenomenon" (Halse & Mowbray, 2011, p. 514). The effect or impact of 'action-oriented' educational research can be observed across a range of spatial and temporal dimensions, from individual classrooms to public policy and the longer-term evolution of initial teacher training (Griffiths, 1998, p. 67). It is hoped that by engaging with action research as a researching practitioner I, too, can have an impact on practice that goes beyond solely the classroom where *praxis* is marked, and into the wider academic community, thus having a positive impact on *theoria*. These hopes and aspirations are bordered by the same sense of trepidation and efficacious doubts outlined earlier in the chapter; however, it is the scaffolding of community and collaboration that is provided by the EdD pathway that allows me to move forward towards the more distant goal of impact on both *praxis* and *theoria*.

Despite the strength of the argument presented supporting my position within the research itself, it is clear from my professional experience across three contrasting secondary school settings that I am in a distinct minority as a practitioner who is driving forward both their own professional development and the improvement of the school's learning environment through educational research. Kayaoglu (2015, p. 141) describes the "scant attention in practice" that the concept of action research as practiced by an in-service teacher has received. He suggests that this lack of consideration might be attributed to what teachers perceive is achievable in relation to educational research or, as is more pertinent to the theme of this chapter, teachers' scepticism about the feasibility of research in a system where they are seen as doers rather than investigators of their own contextualised setting. This view is supported by Fullan (1993), who proposes that the way teachers are trained, the way schools are organised and the way the educational hierarchy operates results in a system where the status quo is more likely to remain. Classroom practitioners are now busier than ever; on-going reforms to assessment practices need to be planned, resourced and embedded in to the ever-evolving school setting where there are constantly increasing levels of scrutiny, both internally and externally. I believe that these pressures, in conjunction with the binary judgement of results and teaching performance by many school leaders, encourages teachers to adopt a very narrow view of professional development, one where engagement with educational research to facilitate the development of practice is not considered and, in my personal experience, has even been scorned. In my opinion these negative attitudes towards educational research are short-sighted and naïve, as the ultimate goal of research is "the systematic observation and analysis of developments and changes that eventuate in order to identify the underlying rationale for the action and to make further changes as required based on findings and outcomes" (Burns, 2009, p. 290). To emphasise the responsibility of teachers to engage with research, I refer to the words of Frost and Durrant (2013, p. 1), who state, "improvements in teaching and learning ultimately depend on the action being taken by teachers". However, for both myself and other fledgling research practitioners it is a case of broadening one's field of view to include research methodologies which, I believe, will foster more fertile grounds for professional development through the theorising and research of practice, giving rise to the potential for significant impact on practice. In terms of my current situation as a practitioner, this means giving consideration to how I can utilise research methodologies to create feedback loops that have the potential to positively inform my own practice and that of others, thus generating impact across the wider school community. I believe that it is only by actively engaging with this cyclical process of professional development that growth of personal practice can be achieved, as, without the use of research data to inform my evaluation of the learning environment that I foster, what am I basing my professional judgement on?

I would like to further develop the theme of how, as a professional doctoral student, my mindset has shifted to hold the split-screen focus on both research and practice, holding two separate but interrelated foci in my field of view, by drawing on Griffiths' (1998) use of Donald Schön's (1983) famous metaphor of the swamps of practice contrasted with the high ground of theory. This metaphor is particularly apt for my current standing at the end of my first term as a professional doctoral researcher, as it highlights the separation and hierarchy present between the two sides of the split-screen focus: the swamps of practice and the high ground of theory. Griffiths (1998, p. 34) comments on the "unnecessarily complicated" language of academics and how it is used in conversational style by a relatively small but powerful group of people. This has the potential to puzzle and exclude practitioners, the very people that the research is meant to support, exacerbating this topographical hierarchy and alienating them from research outcomes. The complex way in which research outcomes are packaged and delivered to practitioners in the language of the high ground could provide a valid explanation to support Kayaoglu's perspectives on the lack of practitioner engagement with research, simply due to practitioners' perception of inaccessibility. That said, this hierarchy works both ways, as teachers have their own specialist language which researchers and others from outside of the profession can perceive to be impenetrable. In light of this, I must give careful consideration to my own position between these two polarised sites, and how my position is not simply a utopian middle ground, but a meandering pathway across the harsh and testing landscape of the EdD journey. One of the greatest challenges of navigating this landscape is mediating and levelling any power relations or tensions that exist between theory and practice, and to achieve this I must be relentlessly reflective and make effective use of the strengths and weaknesses of both views outlined in Schön's metaphor, whilst also giving careful consideration to the way I present my substantive findings so that both groups can interpret and benefit from any outcomes.

Practical Tensions and Conflicts

Having outlined and theoretically framed both the strengths and challenges resulting from my position, it is important to consider the practical duality of the two roles that I am attempting to combine, giving rise to the potential for conflict to appear between two very different standpoints; practice and research. Hammersley (2004) outlines two ways in which the tensions between research and other activities can be managed. The first is where research is subordinated to other activities, in this instance practice, where the pursuit of research goals is geared towards other prevailing concerns. This option would allow me to retain focus on professional practice by not allowing research goals to detract from the teaching and learning environment that I put forward. However, a lack of research focus can result in an oversight of critical understanding relating to the falsity of assumptions and underlying processes, thus compromising the research journey and resulting conclusions. The second management option considers research as a specialised activity, pursued in its own right, where, as Hammersley (2004, p. 174) states, "rather than a practitioner temporarily suspending some other activity in order to carry out an investigation, inquiry becomes the primary occupational practice". By giving research goals centre stage and allowing practice to be fostered through the outcomes of tightly defined research objectives, it maximises chances of finding errors and discovering the range of causal factors at work. The second management option is preferable from a specialised inquiry standpoint, as there is the potential for the dissemination of information that is distal from the practical setting from which it was collected and, as such, may be too complex and inaccessible for practitioners to be of use. As a researching practitioner, who aspires to generating impact on both practice and theory, this an important point to note, as the perceived complexity and inaccessibility of the outcomes to practitioners will nullify this goal which counters the ideology of the professional doctorate pathway. This is especially pertinent to my own context where I may face a full range of interest and beliefs about the usefulness of educational research.

These two contrasting forms of managing the tension between inquiry and practice give rise to an important paradox and, in turn, a clear and critical checkpoint in my shift in mindset towards becoming a researching practitioner. Before embarking on the EdD journey I would have managed the tension between the conflicting activities of practice and research by favouring practice, ensuring that any outcomes of changes and developmental practice contributed to my professional well being, arguably to the detriment of research. Now, however, growth in my knowledge, understanding and beliefs that have been fostered during my first term of doctoral study lead me towards the second stance described by Hammersley, where any conflicts are resolved in favour of inquiry. The growth in knowledge, understanding and beliefs has been achieved through the wholehearted and increasingly fertile engagement with the lectures, research communities and my own academic journey through the relevant literature. Each visit to the faculty has yielded positive learning experiences leading to the growth in confidence and the strengthening of self-efficacious beliefs. It has also been rewarding to reflect on the shift in my own internal dialogue, where, at the start of my EdD journey, I was framing all new learning experiences within my own professional context and practice, whereas now I am increasingly framing my learning within the context of my research. These developments have, in turn, supported the shift in mindset towards becoming a researching practitioner that this chapter frames, allowing me to acknowledge and overcome the academic vulnerability posed by the conflict between inquiry and practice, and is one that will require constant thought and reflection if I am to successfully manage these tensions.

Hammersley (2004) discusses Dewey's pragmatism as one of the most influential philosophical movements on notions of action research. He argues against the cognitive detachment of Descartes' thinking, by suggesting that inquiry both arises in and is shaped by the context of human social life and, as such, should feed back into the flow of on-going collective activity that makes up wider society; in my case, schools. I can relate strongly to Dewey's pragmatism as it strikes a strong accord with my own social constructivist pedagogical beliefs about education and the importance of social interaction in the construction of knowledge and understanding. I fervently believe that my position in practice is a strong stance, where educational research is not only successfully conducted, but can also have a significant impact on the methodology of practitioners across a range of educational contexts. Whilst I acknowledge the conflicts between inquiry and practice outlined above, my position within the "flow of on-going collective activity" of practice, at the coalface of pedagogical excavation and innovation, is one of strength as my immersion within the research itself allows me to reflect deeply on the impacts of pedagogical approaches and make adjustments to optimise both the research outcomes and the learning environment.

INSIDER BUT OUTSIDER – RESEARCH AS REFLECTIVE PRACTICE

I vividly remember the self-efficacious doubts that I battled with before entering the faculty for the induction and first lectures. The two-hour car journey from Oxford provided plenty of time for many cycles of self-doubt, reflection and second-guessing what was about to become. At this point I draw strong parallels between my own initial cycles of self-doubt and that of Korthagen and Vasalos (2005), who identify four limiting factors that prevent teachers achieving what they set out to: limiting behaviour, limiting feelings, limiting images and limiting beliefs. Nias (1989) offers a similar perspective, stating that people feel threatened when they face changes that influence their self-image and, as a result, their personal and professional identity. These two comments couldn't be more apposite to me at this foetal stage of doctoral development, as the limiting feelings and beliefs about my abilities, both as a researcher and as a teacher, negatively influenced my self-image, fostering a view of myself as a deficit model as outlined in the introduction. That said, my desire and drive for personal improvement provided the confidence needed to immerse myself in the experiences provided by the first week of events, offering a strong footing from which to move forward. When reflecting on this thought process, it is now clear to me how vital it was for me to experience the same vulnerability and exposure that is felt by the students that I teach as they embark on new learning journeys, reaffirming my position as not just a researching practitioner, but also as a reflective practitioner. Having experienced the vulnerability of a new learning journey first-hand and, in turn, gained an enhanced understanding of support mechanisms and structures that I personally found valuable, it is clear that I have shifted from being a teacher to being a learner; a reflection that can only serve to improve the support I provide to help students overcome initial uncertainties when encountering their own learning challenges.

My idealistic view of the world makes me want to believe that all teachers reflect on their practice and give thought to how they can enhance the quality of the learning environment that they foster; my pragmatic side inquires as to what depth? There is the danger that teachers' reflection on their practice only reveals a narrow view, one that reflects on practice in light of the learning product that it achieves (Elliott, 1991). The thick lens of examination results encourages a contracted view of reflection, where teachers' assessment of successful teaching is solely based on the volume of knowledge and understanding that students leave the classroom with. Although this is a reflection on the syllabus-driven intended learning outcomes, it is not a reflection on pedagogy. I view pedagogy as a reflective process in itself, one that "requires teachers to reflect in as well as on classroom process quite independently from any assessment they make of the quality of learning outcomes" (Elliott, 1991, p. 10). In my teaching practice to-date I now believe that too often my reflection has been superficial in the sense that it has been purely focused on classroom processes relative to the students' learning outcomes. This is not what Elliott perceives reflexivity to be and it has taken the shift in my mindset towards becoming a researching practitioner, catalysed by the engagement with theory and research, for me to be genuinely reflexive on both myself and my practice.

Fostering reflexivity is crucial to doctoral work. A reflexive scholar is one who applies to their own work the same critical stance, the same interrogative questions, and the same refusal to take things for granted as they do with their research data. Developing a reflexive disposition is profoundly about how we might be perpetuating particular kinds of power relationships, by advancing particular ways of naming and discussing people, experiences and events. Reflexivity thus involves critical self-interrogation (Kamler & Thomson, 2006). In order to be truly reflexive at doctoral research level, I must, therefore, not only make effective use of my experience of practice, but also frame these reflections by making use of knowledge that is found in the high ground of theory. Boyd (2014, p. 443) describes how teachers' professional learning can be viewed as an 'interplay' between practical wisdom and published knowledge. Practical wisdom centres upon teachers' experience, social knowledge and practice-driven professional development, much of which is setting specific and context dependent, whereas published knowledge has been researched by experts within a methodologically and ethically sound framework before being documented and scrutinised by other academics. To successfully achieve the 'interplay' described by Boyd, I must give thought to both the practice-derived theory that informs my epistemological view and to my constantly shifting position along the continuum shaped by the theory-practice relationship (Elliott, 1991). I feel that the acknowledgement of the dynamic nature of this relationship is of great importance at this early stage of my doctoral journey, as it provides relative freedom of thought and flexibility for change rather than the pressure of having to make decisions so early on in terms of epistemological framework and methodological intentions.

This leads me to give thought to the issue of knowledge and, in light of my dynamic position on the theory-practice continuum, what knowledge is relevant to my journey as a researching practitioner. Cain (2015) states that there is little overlap between the types of knowledge generated by educational research and those which are needed in teaching. Researchers seek a deep understanding of matters that can be theoretically framed, whereas teachers require knowledge that is derived from a myriad of different domains: students, colleagues, curriculum reforms, subject knowledge, inspection criteria, school and public policy. It is, therefore, of little surprise that published research may not feature on teachers' professional development radar, if at all. To support this view, Levin (2013, p. 12) states that "practitioners in every field give greater weight to the views of their colleagues and their interpretations of their own experience than they do to research evidence". If this is indeed the case, is my attempt to climb out of the swamps of practice to scale the summit of the high ground of theory futile in its nature? Can I usefully and successfully combine research-generated knowledge and pedagogical, practice-generated knowledge? Or, as McIntyre (2005, p. 359) describes it, "sharply contrasting kinds of knowledge"?

To answer this question I refer to the figure below, Figure 1, which identifies five key characteristics for both research generated knowledge and teachers' pedagogical knowledge. In its original form Cain (2015) simply presented this information as a table, but I have displayed it as converging arrows for the two contrasting types of knowledge, emphasising the meeting of these opposing units of knowledge on my own research journey; a meeting that fortifies the researching practitioner's view of knowledge pertinent to doctoral study. This method of data presentation also allows me to visually express the shift in mindset, as my position before embarking on my professional doctorate journey was towards the right of centre, with only limited awareness of the different forms of research generated knowledge. Now, however, in adjusting my field of view to include the high ground of research-generated knowledge, my position has shifted towards the central confluence of the two modes of knowledge. That said, my current standing at this early stage of my doctoral journey is right of centre as, although I am actively engaging with the research generated knowledge of *theoria*, my thought process is, as Levin suggests, more strongly governed by my interpretations of my professional experience to-date. As is the theme throughout this reflective chapter, my position is not simply a polarised one where my mindset has fundamentally shifted from one end of the theory-practice continuum to the other; instead I must accept that my learning and academic growth will shift me along this continuum and I believe the metacognitive reflection on and understanding of this movement is of vital importance to the successful conflation of these two stances. The movement along this continuum over the course of my first term of doctoral study is more accurately represented in Figure 2, highlighting the movement from a purely practice outlook to one that includes theory, towards the end goal of the mindset of a researching practitioner.

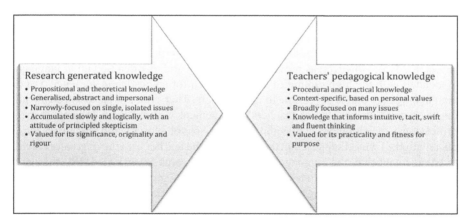

Figure 1. A summary of different types of knowledge influencing my position as a researching practitioner (adapted from Cain, 2015, p. 494)

It is important to note that the confluence of the two different types of knowledge resulting from the shift in mindset outlined above is not free from challenge. Procter (2015) highlights two difficulties with teachers using evidence gained from research on which to base their practice. The first is that teachers have concerns over the quality, relevance and accessibility of research in education to practitioners and the second is that teachers report a high level of receptivity to research but a relatively low level of active engagement with research. Clearly, if research is to be used by

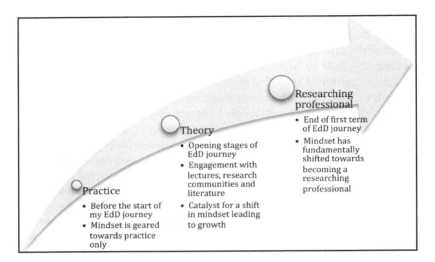

Figure 2. A continuum of the shift in mindset during my first
term of professional doctorate study

teachers it needs to be both relevant and accessible to practitioners, so that they can make effective use of its findings and allow it to inform pedagogical development (Procter, 2015). However, as previously stated, research is often tied up in language associated with the high ground of theory, written for an academic audience, rather than in language that is accessible to practitioners. That said, I have observed a wide range of mindsets relating to teachers' engagement with research to support their professional development across the different school settings and, based on these observations, I would suggest that the mindset of the teacher provides a greater barrier to engagement than the language in which the research is packaged. Practitioners' indifference towards research could be attributed to some of the thoughts shared earlier in the chapter relating to perceived business, scrutiny and judgement by senior management and, above all, the nature and structure of professional development practices that operate within different school settings. Perhaps research is seen as an unnecessary add-on to their already bulging professional offerings? Perhaps they perceive the development of practice solely through reflection on practice and the sharing of professional experience?

To answer these questions I draw on ideas shared by Apelgren et al. (2015) who state that theory use is central to professional efforts for quality of practice. This is supported by Ingerman and Wickman (2015) who state that transforming teaching practice is the fusion of research outcomes with current teaching and learning practices into new professional practices. After only one term of doctoral study I am already sensing growth in my professional practice; however, in order to achieve impact beyond just my own classroom I must give thought and consideration to not just the research process itself but also the way in which the outcomes are packaged to allow them to be accessible, engaging and far-reaching. Levin (2013, p. 2) has defined knowledge mobilisation as: "efforts to understand and strengthen the relationship between research and practice". I propose that this view forms an accurate summary of my role as a researching practitioner, as my position, drawing on the strengths of both research and practice, allows me to foster and develop this relationship. As such, the strengthening of the relationship between research and practice forms a significant aim for me to work towards, measured after five years by the scale of the impact that my journey has had on the swamps of practice – a ripple or a splash?

CLOSING REFLECTIONS

One of the underlying continuing themes of this chapter is that different theories can support researchers in understanding overt and underlying structures in order to be able to act and navigate the complexities and anxieties related to doctoral research. Similarly argued, but in the context of supporting teachers, Apelgren et al. (2015, p. 8) state that 'proper' research is grounded in practice, based on theory and informed by knowledge and reflections. This chapter has provided a reflexive and theoretically framed account of the fundamental shift in mindset that I experienced over my first term as a Doctor of Education student. This shift has moved me from a narrow outlook of the educational landscape, solely focused on practice, towards a view where I have been able to observe and learn the theories and behaviours of a researching practitioner. In theorising this shift I have used the relevant literature to critically evaluate the perceived strengths and weaknesses of my constantly changing position along the continuum shown in Figure 2, as I have taken my first exploratory steps along my doctoral journey. In this sense I have engaged with 'proper' research. That said, the professional doctoral landscape is a harsh and intimidating one, creating opportunities for efficacious doubt and uncertainties with regard to the knowledge required to be successful. However I, like Andrews and Edwards (2008), have begun to move through this landscape with confidence, making small inroads into my long, five-year journey. I *am* becoming a researching practitioner.

This chapter attempts to make a significant contribution to both this book and the "Critical issues in the future of learning and teaching" series. It has been authored by a novice researcher, at the foetal stage of development in terms of my own knowledge, understanding and abilities and, as such, has provided the context for the transformative nature of the shift in mindset that I have experienced towards becoming a researching professional engaged in and construing professional doctoral research as that which derives from professional experience and expertise. It is hoped that this chapter provides support, both metacognitive and emotional, to other doctoral students who are embarking on their own professional doctorate journeys. In light of this I would like to share three challenges for both new and perspective researching professionals to consider at the start of their own journeys:

1. *Be constantly reflective* – It is vital to consider the dynamic nature of your position as a researching practitioner between the swamps of practice and the high ground of theory (Schön, 1983). Draw on the strengths of both positions whilst retaining a sound understanding of the limitations and conflicts that might arise.
2. *Network with and make full and effective use of the research communities around you* – One of the greatest strengths of the Doctorate of Education pathway is the sense of community provided by the collaborative learning environment of professionals. You are not alone on your journey and I recommend making full use of the 'social' resources that will support your progress.
3. *Relish the challenges that the journey brings* – Combining a full-time teaching job with doctoral study is a huge challenge in itself. When you add to that the pressures outlined in the introduction, describing the need to create new knowledge that leads to impact in the field, the challenges grow in size considerably. It is vital to relish challenge in whatever form it takes. Believe in yourself and your abilities as a researching professional; each step, no matter how small, *is* progress.

This writing experience has been a hugely powerful and developmental one for me. It has not only provided the opportunity to re-engage with academic writing not undertaken since the completion of my Masters' thesis, but it has also encouraged me to be truly reflexive by stepping back from my initial progress across the vast ocean of doctoral study and observing the extent of the shift in my mindset towards becoming a researching practitioner. Having successfully navigated the stormy waters of self-doubt and the perception of myself as a deficit model during the opening stages of my five-year journey, I am now moving forward with confidence. Despite the countless academic and practical challenges that lie ahead, I am genuinely excited about making further progress on my professional doctorate journey and look forward to the personal growth and professional impact that this expedition will have, both on my practice and that of others.

REFERENCES

Andrews, D., & Edwards, C. (2008). Consciousness in transition: The experience of doctoral study. In B. Cunningham (Ed.), *Exploring professionalism*. London: Institute of Education, University of London.

Apelgren, B. M., Burnard, P., & Cabaroglu, N. (2015). Theory-use in teacher research. In P. Burnard, B. M. Apelgren, & N. Cabaroglu (Eds.), *Transformative teacher research: Theory and practice for the C21st* (pp. 3–12). Rotterdam, The Netherlands: Sense Publishers.

Boyd, P. (2014). Learning conversations: Teacher researchers evaluating dialogic strategies in early years settings. *International Journal of Early Years Education, 22*(4), 441–456.

Bruner, J. S. (1986). *Actual minds, possible worlds*. Cambridge, MA & London: Harvard University Press.

Burns, A. (2009). Action research in second language teacher education. In J. C. Richards & A. Burns (Eds.), *The Cambridge guide to second language teacher education* (pp. 289–297). Cambridge: Cambridge University Press.

Cain, T. (2015). Teachers' engagement with published research: Addressing the knowledge problem. *Curriculum Journal, 26*(3), 488–509.

Elliott, J. (1991). *Action research for educational change*. Buckingham: Open University Press.

Fang, F., Kang, S.-P., & Liu, S. (2004). *Measuring mindset change in the systemic transformation of education*. Association for Educational Communications and Technology, 27th, Chicago, IL.

Frost, D., & Durrant, J. (2013). *Teacher-led development work: Guidance and support*. London: Routledge.

Fullan, M. (1993). Why teachers must become change agents. *Educational Leadership, 50*(5), 1–13.

Griffiths, M. (1998). *Educational research for social justice: Getting off the fence*. London: McGraw-Hill Education.

Halse, C., & Mowbray, S. (2011). The impact of the doctorate. *Studies in Higher Education, 36*(5), 513–525.

Hammersley, M. (2004). Action research: A contradiction in terms? *Oxford Review of Education, 30*(2), 165–181.

Ingerman, A., & Wickman, P.-O. (2015). Towards a teachers' professional discipline. In P. Burnard, B. M. Apelgren, & N. Cabaroglu (Eds.), *Transformative teacher research: Theory and practice for the C21st* (pp. 167–179). Rotterdam, The Netherlands: Sense Publishers.

Kamler, B., & Thomson, P. (2006). *Helping doctoral students write: Pedagogies for supervision*. London: Routledge.

Kayaoglu, M. N. (2015). Teacher researchers in action research in a heavily centralized education system. *Educational Action Research, 23*(2), 140–161.

Korthagen, F. A. J., & Vasalos, A. (2005). Levels in reflection: Core reflection as a means to enhance professional growth. *Teachers & Teaching, 11*(1), 47–71.

Levin, B. (2013). To know is not enough: Research knowledge and its use. *Review of Education, 1*(1), 2–31.

McIntyre, D. (2005). Bridging the gap between research and practice. *Cambridge Journal of Education, 1*(1), 2–31.

McKernan, J. (1996). *Curriculum action research: A handbook of methods and resources for the reflective practitioner* (2nd ed.). London: Kogan Page.

Morrissey, D. (2014). An autoethnographic inquiry into the role of serendipity in becoming a teacher educator/researcher. *International Journal of Qualitative Studies in Education, 27*(7), 837–849.

Nias, J. (1989). *Primary teachers talking: A study of teaching as work*. London: Routledge.

Palmer, P. J. (2007). *The courage to teach: Exploring the inner landscape of a teacher's life* (10th anniversary). San Francisco, CA & Chichester: Jossey-Bass; John Wiley.

Procter, R. (2015). Teachers and school research practices: The gaps between the values and practices of teachers. *Journal of Education for Teaching, 41*(5), 464–477.

Schön, D. A. (1983). *The reflective practitioner: How professionals think in action*. New York, NY: Basic Books.

Somekh, B. (1994). Inhabiting each other's castles: Towards knowledge and mutual growth through collaboration. *Educational Action Research, 2*(3), 357–381.

Stenhouse, L. (1975). *An introduction to curriculum research and development*. London: Heinemann.

Walford, G. (1991). *Doing educational research*. London: Routledge.

JAMES EDWARD KNOWLES

7. PROFESSIONAL DOCTORATE RESEARCHING AND THE CHANGING 'SELF'

A Personal and Professional Journey

INTRODUCTION

This chapter addresses the issue of becoming a professional doctorate researcher and the changing 'self'. Taking a sociological perspective I draw on theories of Bourdieu and Foucault to consider why we should ask, who are we or who do we become? Both scholars assert that who we are or who we become depends on social interactions and that we change through our experiences of the social world around us. Whilst Bourdieu focuses on how macro-social stratification such as social class determines who we are and limits who we may become, Foucault avoids acknowledging such categorisations, instead emphasising that there is no innate self and that which others call 'the self' is entirely constituted through social interactions. By reflecting on Foucault's (Gutting, 2005) 'self', Bourdieu's (Crossley, 2008; Reed-Danahay, 2005) 'habitus' and on my own personal experiences of doing a professional doctorate, I offer insight into what becoming a doctor of education is like and how it is experienced subjectively.

The line of argument that threads through this chapter is that through learning we change as people, mostly in the positive ways anticipated, but also in less certain or predictable ways. I argue that acquiring a qualification does not mean, simply, that we are the same person who now has a certificate, a ticket to another job for instance, but that the process of learning through doctoral research as well as struggling with ideas and against adversities, affect who we become, as well.

I argue that the personal and professional journeys are entwined through lifelong learning. I also assert that these two categories, the professional and the personal, although distinguishable are inseparable. At the nexus between the multiple dimensions of our lives lies the 'self'. To me, the key to continually developing personally and professionally is to be reflexive and become adaptable to ever changing environments. Recognising that the educational landscape will always be changing, and that to survive in an unpredictable environment requires acceptance of the changing self, is inevitable. The professional doctorate in education provides the perfect opportunity for me, as an experienced and aspirational science teacher, to undertake a study of personal and professional interest that will ultimately change 'the self' in a way of my own choosing.

P. Burnard et al. (Eds.), Transformative Doctoral Research Practices for Professionals, 91–100.

THEORISING THE SELF: WHO WE ARE AND WHO WE BECOME

From my own experience as a physics teacher, who we are and who we become depends on many things. Some of us recognise talents or gifts we may have early on in life and some of us take time to realise them. In order to recognise what we do well, we need to have the opportunity to try them in the first place. For me, as it might be for many others, my journey was influenced by my family, and yet who we become depends, as well, on our own personal agency, that is, what we strive for and how we make it happen. While one's background counts for a lot, not everyone lives in the same social situation or experiences the same 'habitus'.

'The Self': According to Bourdieu

Bourdieu's 'habitus' conceives how different social classes produce certain lifestyles. These include how highly they value education, what television programmes they watch, what music they listen to, what food they eat and who they associate with. So 'habitus' reflects the way different classes perceive the world around them and understand it, indicating their preferred tastes. Habitus has a structure, yet it structures daily lives (Haralambos & Holborn, 2004, p. 67).

> According to Bourdieu, habitus is an internalised, embodied disposition toward the world. It comes into being through inculcation in early childhood, which is not a process of deliberate, formal teaching and learning but, rather, one associated with immersion in a particular social milieu – the family and the household. (Reed-Danahay, 2005, p. 46)

So, who we are depends to some extent on whom we mix with, as does who we become. Although the latter is also influenced through personal agency, some social circumstances place hurdles in front of those from the lower classes striving to improve their social positioning. For instance we have no choice about the family we are born into, which means that 'economic' and 'cultural' capitals vary widely between individuals. Those who have high capital will tend to find it easier to accumulate more.

So, to summarise the lesson I take from Bourdieu, we are who we are born to be, yet we become who we *choose* to become, within our means. As the son of two teachers, I was brought up to value education highly. My father Norman Knowles, (pseudonym: Trevor Wood) was a 'Young worker at College', researched by Venables (1967), from whom, along with my mother Margaret, I have drawn a lifetime of inspiration.

> Wood is an extreme case – though not an isolated one – of the chaps who know that Grammar School and University are not the only means of 'getting what you want'. They are not necessarily motivated in any specific way – they have grown up to think that studying and getting a certificate is a good thing to do;

an attitude socially induced – like other attitudes – by parents, friend, teacher, or who knows who. (Venables, 1967, pp. 66–67)

Through a lifetime of learning I like to think that each qualification I have chosen to gain has made me a better and wiser person. So to me learning has always been about self-improvement acquired through a curiosity of the world. For this reason I have chosen to embark on the professional doctorate in education to attain the highest qualification available for an educator but also, and most importantly, to become the person I want to be. Through my professional doctorate journey, I am coming to realise that living life through work and bridging practice and research, while aspiring for self-improvement, is helping me to become someone else. This resonates with me as I accept that life is a journey of self-discovery, a mission in finding oneself, repeatedly questioning who we are and what we stand for, yet accepting that the answers to these questions and 'the self' might not ever be found or fixed.

'The Self': According to Foucault

Foucault offers understanding about how society operates in context, through *discourses* and *power* relations that shape us all. Foucault uses "discourse to mean taken-for-granted 'rules' that specify what is possible to speak, do and even think, at a particular time" (Walshaw, 2007, p. 19). "Discourses for [Foucault] refer to different ways of structuring knowledge[;] immensely powerful [because] they produce truths" (Walshaw, 2007, p. 19). Through discourses *selves* are situated in jointly produced story lines (Gonsalves & Seiler, 2012, p. 159). Through discourse people become positioned amongst others, not necessarily intentionally (Gonsalves & Seiler, 2012, p. 159). This "positioning can be interactive whereby one positions another, or reflexive, wherein one positions oneself" (Gonsalves & Seiler, 2012, p. 159).

My choice to embark on a professional doctorate in education was a decision to position myself as a researching professional in the context of physics teaching and further education. The professional discourses as a physics teacher and as a professional doctorate student enabled me to engage with my own interests as a researcher but also with educational discourses that position the learners' perspectives as agents of their own learning. The role of the research in relation to others is both important and empowering. As course leader I undoubtedly hold a position of traditional power over my students. As I (and my colleagues) write the course, teach it and assess it, the students, on the whole, are eager to please us. Whilst recognising this, Foucault teaches us that power can be enacted productively, and that it is perhaps most effective when enacted as such. "Where there is power, there is resistance" (Foucault, 1978, p. 95), so it makes sense to limit the enacting of oppressive power such as the use of sanctions, where enacting of productive power such as persuasion to do the right thing, can be used instead. This may not always be easy but taking a Foucaultian approach to leadership involves making persuasive arguments, as we do through research, not only to limit the likelihood or frequency of resistance, but to empower those we lead to become well educated potential leaders of the future. Foucault teaches us that power and knowledge are inseparable. Through encouraging our students to think for themselves and to challenge taken for granted truths, they can be encouraged to lead more fulfilled lives becoming agents of influence in their own lives, as opposed to becoming "fabricated by (the discourses of) others" (Walshaw, 2007, p. 16). For me being a teacher-researcher, a researching professional teaching and leading, now involves avoiding dominating discourses wherever possible, so as to encourage all to prosper. It also involves being honest about where teaching, leading and researching overlap and making this transparent to students where possible. It is also important to promote the research as benefiting teachers and students on a wider scale, so that the students can glimpse beyond the immediacy of the teacher in charge.

> In Foucaultian research, learners are the product of the discourses and practices through which they become subjected. (Walshaw, 2007, p. 70)

Learning from Foucault I advise teacher-researchers to challenge dominant political discourses, such as competition, being the natural way of learning and governing. Although striving to improve is important, where there are winners there are losers, so despite the relative successes of others we should encourage our students to resist becoming subjected to categorisation as losers responsible for their own failure, as promoted through oppressive discourses that blind us to the structural advantages our so-called competitors may hold over us.

For Foucault, "power induces pleasure as well as producing knowledge" (Foucault, 1980, p. 119). Through the Access to Medicine course, some of the students I researched described 'a love of learning' as a major motivator in wanting to acquire a holistic understanding of the sciences, highlighting that pleasure can be induced through the power of education. Moreover for prospective medicine students, knowledge becomes constructed as the power to educate and cure, (Foucault, 1977, p. 303) emphasising how power can operate productively and progressively, to produce more professional knowledge through lifelong learning. So power-knowledge becomes inseparable.

So, to summarise Foucault, we situate 'the self' and enact power relations through discourses. In order to analyse how the self and power operate through these discourses, we need to consider the context in which we function both personally and professionally.

PLACING MY DOCTORAL RESEARCH IN ITS PROFESSIONAL CONTEXT

Through my doctoral thesis, I tell the stories of my students as they progress through the 'Access to Medicine' course at a college of Further Education (FE). The sector of Further Education is located between the compulsory secondary or high school sector and higher (university) education sectors. Historically, the FE sector has run courses to provide school leavers and adults with the skills required to work in local industries. Panchamia (2012, p. 1) refers to it as the 'everything else' sector due to the wide breadth of provision offered by such institutions. However FE colleges are perhaps best known for their lead role in vocational education (Schuller & Watson, 2009, p. 18). My research aims to conduct a discourse analysis of the narratives of would-be-medical doctors for the purpose of theorising the role of power evidenced in their learning journeys.

The specific course that I teach is called Access to Medicine and Dentistry. This includes the teaching of physics and general research methods, required for the completion of students' self-chosen research projects. I teach this to Level 3 which is equivalent to A-Level.[1]

My journey from being a secondary school physics teacher to an Further Education teacher originated from my longing to acquire a holistic understanding of Physics at a higher level, in order to construct a more advanced professional knowledge of teaching it so as to influence prospective medicine students, who could potentially make full use of such knowledge through enacting their power to cure.

The journey continues with the professional doctorate in education because it provides the perfect opportunity for me, as an experienced and aspirational teacher, to undertake a study of personal interest that will develop me professionally, and ultimately change 'the self'.

Professional doctorate research offers teachers who continue to teach, as a full time job, and wish to research their own practice, an opportunity to re-invent their teacher-selves through taking control of their own professional development. In their seminal work, Thomson and Walker (Thomson & Walker, 2010, p. 390), argue that doctoral researchers are faced with many decisions that involve self, positioning, power and discourses of all research stakeholders. They alert us to the fact that methodologies are more than matters of technique, and that the point of the thesis is to add new knowledge which we disseminate in both scholarly and public fora.

In order to add new knowledge we need to first comprehend much of what is already known in a very specific area, in order to identify a unique avenue of enquiry. This requires reading, yet, from my experience, this changes the self through learning to take on board a new theoretical perspective, which may not have previously been available to us, and which is also adaptable to the context of the research.

Thomson and Walker (Thomson & Walker, 2010, p. 392) also suggest "that all doctoral researchers [should be] encouraged to ask unsettling questions about their research" including questions about the underpinning assumptions about the world, to what ends are they directed, in whose interests they work and what kinds of knowledges are being produced? Being reflexive, raising political, ontological and epistemological questions is crucial. However, Thomson and Walker (2010, p. 393) provide a helpful health warning to not over-emphasise the finding of new knowledge but rather to be more balanced with the inclusion of what they refer to as "a new voice in the conversation, a different angle and slant on something that many are concerned about" (Thomson & Walker, 2010, pp. 392–393). For me, this means that although Thomson and Walker (2010) advocate that doctoral research in the social sciences should address current public concerns, this should not be misinterpreted to mean that all doctoral research must be disseminated to the public directly. The extent to which doctoral research contributes to academic or public fora depends on what kind of research it is. An important consideration for researching professionals in education, as I am, is that we can influence our students through what we have learnt during professional doctorate research. So when Thomson and Walker (2010) state that "research-led teaching is a goal not to be passed over in the search for contribution" (p. 394), I feel that through professional doctorate research, I am leading my students by example, becoming more educated myself through researching. Whilst practicing what I teach in my research methods lessons, I prepare the students to become more independent in their learning, through completing their own research project for the Access to Medicine and Dentistry' course.

To me, professional doctorate research is about changing thinking, about how we do things, thinking about who we are, who we want to become, how we can do things better and even how we can live more fulfilled lives. For example I used to see myself as a teacher of physics, preparing students for applying their knowledge through engineering to develop society, whilst I remained somewhat independent of the teacher in me. Through embarking on a professional doctorate I now see myself as a researching professional who is engaged with reflexive research-based teaching, leading a professional learning community in order to collaboratively develop students' perspectives on practice and inquiry, along with discipline and engagement of action within an ever changing society.

Some of what I write, I hope, will contribute to academic fora, making me recognisable as a researching professional. This journey has helped me to resolve problems of practice and provide evidence for change. For example initial findings from my research suggest that those students who have not been to university – those students Access courses are designed for – tend to be the ones who struggle the most with completing their university applications, showing that more support from the college for these students would be helpful. This could be disseminated through 'Access Validating Agencies' who run similar courses, in order for students to benefit from the findings directly without needing to refer to the full findings from the thesis. However there is a limit to how much staff from any college can support students new to them, through a one month application process that many A-level students, that the system was designed for, may have taken a year over, without support from teachers who may know them very well. Hence findings more directly related to the academic research questions will be better disseminated through academic fora so that insights gained from the specific theoretical perspective can be appreciated more widely by the academic community, to influence policy makers.

It may be that some of my research will be disseminated through social media, through presentations, scholarly peer reviewed journal articles, conference presentations. However, as I am positioned both as a public servant and a doctoral researching professional, I can directly and immediately influence those with whom I engage through my research and professional context. As mentioned previously I have led by example as a researching professional, whilst engaging with learners in interviews. This I feel is respected by the students who recognise the effort being put into not only the researcher's professional development, but also the leading of students like them. Moreover it is what will be found from the thesis findings along with how I have changed through the process of writing it, which will provide food for thought, to develop the course for future cohorts.

So I argue that doing a professional doctorate is as much about personal development as it is about professional development. Yet they are forever entwined. Attempting to develop the professional will change the personal, as learning to think reflexively allows us to question what we do, why we do things, who we are and who we want to become, which cannot easily be compartmentalised into separated strands of our lives. This type of researcher positioning changes my sense of self as a researching professional. I am shifting, from seeing myself as a qualified teacher to a professional who researches his own practice and, hopefully, becomes an experienced researching professional who bridges research and practice. But how has doctoral researching changed me?

HOW MY DOCTORAL JOURNEY HAS CHANGED ME

Through engaging in a professional doctorate to improve my professional practice, changes occurred which affected my personal, as well as my professional, selves. Embarking on the Doctorate of Education, I set out to find out why fewer women choose to study Advanced level Physics than men in the context of a Further Education College in England. The fundamental flaw with this gender-focused question was the assumption that it has a simple answer. I was advised that the project focus had to change. I was led to the work of Michel Foucault. His words, such as "the main interest in life and work is to become someone else that you were not in the beginning" – cited in (Gutting, 2005, p. 6) – resonated with me. This statement impacted on me most strongly, because it summarised my reasons for starting and continuing with the professional doctorate journey. I came to see that in order to exercise some power within my own life, and grasp at gaining some agency at this point, it was essential to change the way I was thinking about my professional doctorate research. Foucault (1972) helped me, with his famous words "don't ask me who I am and don't ask me to remain the same" (p. 17); I came to see that one can overcome setbacks and engage reflexively with advice. Once I recognised the significance of theory, notions of power and conceptions of self, I felt empowerment. I began to take new steps in putting forward my aims as a professional and as researcher. I kept asking questions about who has the power and whose voices will the research represent. I learned that I can change myself and develop alternative paths using Foucault as my guide.

Telling the 'Access to Medicine' students' stories, as referred to earlier, my research began to amplify my thinking in new and different ways. I began to recognise that the people around me related to me differently, in my new role as a researching professional.

As in many lives, much of what is lived is not planned nor anticipated. The big surprise, for me, taking on employment in Further Education, meant a reduction in income in order to allow me the space to develop as a researching professional. More comfortable in this role than any other in my career, however, I started to develop the self I did not know before. However, it did not come without costs, both financial and emotional.

After my first year at the college before embarking on the professional doctorate journey, three-hour return daily commutes were taking their toll on my family and me. Despite returning home every evening, I was soon in bed resting for the next day, leaving little time and space to enjoy family life in the way I had envisaged it. Whilst ecstatic to have gained a place on the University of Cambridge's first 'Doctorate in Education' cohort, it was immediately necessary to give up the daily commutes and take lodging with a friend. This meant that the time that would have been spent driving could be spent reading for the doctorate, not losing too much of the benefits of family habitus, especially at evening time, whilst still being able to have a family life at the weekend. Both professional habitus and personal habitus were disrupted. But this was not the end of the setbacks and processes of changing self.

What followed was a series of financial cut backs at the college. This meant that after the second year, funding was no longer available for my professional doctorate. This coincided with the upheaval of having nowhere to lodge. This forced me to make several more changes, including the change of status from a funded doctoral path to a self-funded one. And there was another change. I had to set up a multipurpose vehicle (MPV) as a camper van and sleep in it overnight through the following Summer and Autumn terms. I had to exercise power and agency in a new unexpected and undesirable habitus. I found I had to give myself more time to think, to reflect and to re-engage with the research. As a consequence of all of these changes, I felt a deep loneliness which manifested itself in the need to take time out to reflect on the making of new calculations, new actions, new discourses, new contexts. I came to understand that out of adversity, comes a change of self. Lack of funds to fuel daily commutes, needing to feed a family and remain committed to the professional doctorate journey upon which I had embarked, demonstrated to me Foucault's notion of "power operates from everywhere". Within the constraints, I came to feel empowered by these new meanings and the possibility of moving into new spaces and finding new solutions. Indeed I chose to enter into a partial life of monastic vagrancy – what for many would seem 'odd' and in Foucaultian terms 'abnormal'; I chose to operate power in this way in order to take back some control of my own life and carry on with my aspiration of becoming a doctor from perhaps the most prestigious university in the world. I looked for, created and renewed motivations in spite of, in Bourdieusian terms, lacking *economic capital* (Crossley, 2008, p. 90); I remained steadfast. I took on additional employment, privately tutoring for two companies, which further took time away from my studies and my family life. Through my nomadic lifestyle I have drawn strength from my own family and others, whilst learning to cope with loneliness and poverty. This has developed me personally and professionally.

As a professional doctorate researcher I now enact my reflexivity through questioning who I am and accepting that I am changing. I am sharing my research experiences of the ever-changing self. Using the principles learned through the adversity and evolution of my research, I now practice a reflexive approach and I celebrate the fact that my research is meant to bring about precisely such change, both personally and professionally. This is what drives the rest of my doctoral journey.

CLOSING REFLECTIONS

I hope some of my lessons relate to your journey and challenge the reader. We often take for granted what we think we know about ourselves. It is through the struggle of research that I gain new perspectives and that I learn from my ever changing self. Recognising my own vulnerability through writing my story, I hope to convey how the personal and professional selves are entwined and that power operates through both.

Professional doctorate researching is a transformative practice in and of itself. Reflecting on my own personal and professional journey allowed me to see how this transformative practice contributed to my changing self. As I took back the controls to navigate my own way, I overcame many setbacks. What I have learned from writing this chapter is a set of guiding principles for writing as a researching professional. These are rooted in considerations of voice, reflexivity, uncertainty and vulnerability, at all stages of research from getting started to dissemination and taking responsibility as members of the wider community of researching professionals.

NOTE

[1]   The A Level, is a secondary school (non-compulsory) leaving qualification offered in England, Wales and Northern Ireland. Obtaining A Level is generally a pre-condition for university entrance.

REFERENCES

Crossley, N. (2008). 5 Social class. In P. Bourdieu (Ed.), *Key concepts* (p. 248). Stocksfield: Acumen Publishing Limited.
Foucault, M. (1972). *The archaeology of knowledge* (1st ed.). London: Routledge.
Foucault, M. (1977). *Discipline and punish* (1st ed.). London: Penguin.
Foucault, M. (1978). *The history of sexuality: 1 the will to knowledge* (1st ed., Vol. 1). London: Penguin.
Foucault, M. (1980). *Power/Knowledge: Selected interviews and other writings 1972–1977* (1st ed.). Harlow: Harvester Press. Retrieved from http://www.pearsoned.co.uk

Gonsalves, A. J., & Seiler, G. (2012). 11. Recognising 'Smart Super-Physicists': Gendering competence in Doctoral Physics. In M. Varelas (Ed.), *Identity construction and science education research learning, teaching, and being in multiple contexts* (p. 189). New York, NY: Springer-Verlag.

Gutting, G. (2005). *Foucault: A very short introduction.* Oxford: Oxford University Press.

Haralambos, M., & Holborn, M. (2004). *Sociology themes and perspectives* (6th ed.). London: Harper Collins.

Panchamia, N. (2012). *Choice and competition in further education* (p. 9). London: Institute for Government. Retrieved from http://www.instituteforgovernment.org.uk/sites/default/files/publications/FE%20Briefing%20final.pdf

Reed-Danahay, D. (2005). *Locating Bourdieu.* Bloomington, IN & Indianapolis, IN: Indiana University Press.

Schuller, T., & Watson, D. (2009). *FE colleges in a new culture of adult and lifelong learning* (No. 7) (p. 79). Leicester: Inquiry into the Future for Lifelong Learning. Retrieved from http://www.niace.org.uk/lifelonglearninginquiry/docs/IFLL-Sector-paper7.pdf

Thomson, P., & Walker, M. (2010). Why doctoral study? In P. Thomson & M. Walker (Eds.), *The Routledge doctoral student's companion: Getting to grips with research in Education and the social sciences* (1st ed., p. 425). London & New York, NY: Routledge.

Venables, E. (1967). *The young worker at college a study of a local tech* (1st ed.). London: Faber and Faber Ltd.

Walshaw, M. (2007). *Working with Foucault in education* (1st ed.). Rotterdam, The Netherlands/Taipei: Sense Publishers. Retrieved from http://www.sensepublishers.com

DENISE WHALLEY

8. MOVING FROM PRACTITIONER TO RESEARCHING PROFESSIONAL

Shifts of Identity

INTRODUCTION

This chapter considers models for the transition of professional doctorate students from practitioner to researcher, examining the process of synthesising different perspectives and identities and exploring some of the conflicts that can arise when theory challenges practice.

The motivation of those who enter professional doctoral programmes (in this book the Doctorate of Education, or EdD) is "not to explore an abstract question, or follow a whim. Instead, their mission as doctoral students is, overwhelmingly, to improve schools" (Labaree, 2003, p. 16). Educational scholarship, through pursuing a doctoral programme, will enable the students to "develop research findings – concepts, generalization, theories – that make sense of educational processes across contexts and offer them to teachers and other practitioners" (Labaree, 2003, p. 20).

However, experienced practitioners bring the perspective of professional experience, sometimes gained over many years. The median age of those receiving an EdD in the US in 2003 was 44 (Labaree, 2003, p. 15), implying the influence of years of professional practice in education or related fields. Their identities as practitioners have been established, tested and strengthened over time. This means that, while at the start of the programmes students hold strong "perceptions of themselves as learners and leaders, they do not hold prominent perceptions of themselves as researchers" (Buss et al., 2014, p. 137).

Fenge poses the question to those embarking upon professional doctorates: "Where do practitioner roles stop and research and practice development begin?" (Fenge, 2010, p. 650). There is no simple answer to this, no sudden change in identity when the professional doctorate student suddenly becomes a researcher not a practitioner: but this chapter aims to explore the different models of identity and how they combine and shift.

In this chapter, I draw on two bodies of literature:

• The transition from education practitioner to researching professional: shifts in thinking that can aid this transition.

P. Burnard et al. (Eds.), Transformative Doctoral Research Practices for Professionals, 101–111.

- The identity of the professional doctorate student as professional practitioner and researcher: how can these be merged and synthesised so that the result is amplified?

By mapping incidents through my own transition from experienced practitioner to early-stage researcher, I explore the ways in which theory improved my professional practice and initiated the transition from practitioner to researcher, yet ultimately challenged and changed my identity as a school leader.

The three sections of this chapter are broadly chronological:

- Part One explores my identity as an experienced practitioner.
- Part Two uses a framework proposed by Labaree (2003) to explore the transition from practitioner to researching professional.
- Part Three revisits identity as an emerging researching professional.

Throughout the chapter, I position myself as a 'Chair of Governors', and will briefly explain this below, while acknowledging that this is a position that is not well recognised outside the English educational system. However the issues considered in this chapter will resonate with those who are in positions of strategic (as opposed to operational) school leadership, and those who take the role of chairing strategic steering groups in any sector.

PART ONE: PROFESSIONAL IDENTITY

My role within the English education system, at the time of starting my doctoral study, was that of a Chair of Governors. All schools have a Governing Board – a small group of committed volunteers, drawn from the school, parents, the local community and representatives from the sponsoring authority. The role of governors has changed over time, but, broadly, is to act as critical friends, to challenge and support the school, and to reassure the wider community that public money is being spent responsibly in the best interests of the children's education.

Traditionally, governors have held a supportive position within the school. Themes from 1978, where most governors "subscribed to what might best be called an ethic of community service and simply wanted to become involved with, and help in whatever way was possible, the work of their local school" (Bacon, 1978, p. 84) are still echoed in governance literature today, more recently "characterised by a deep-seated desire to contribute, an attachment to education and/or their school, and a desire to improve society generally through education" (James et al., 2013a, p. 15).

However, school governance is undergoing a fundamental period of change in England at the moment as a result of reforms in national educational policy. Top-down changes imposed by successive governments since 2010 have brought governors into the accountability framework of English educational policy and placed them alongside the head teacher (school principal) as part of a school's strategic leadership structure. As a consequence of this, the core tasks of a school governor are now:

1. *Ensuring clarity of vision, ethos and strategic direction;*
2. *Holding the head teacher to account for the educational performance of the school and its pupils, and the performance management of staff; and*
3. *Overseeing the financial performance of the school and making sure its money is well spent* (Department for Education, 2015, p. 7).

This significant change, implemented over the relatively short period of five years, has posed a challenge for all governors, particularly Chairs who are required to develop the necessary skills to govern and lead the schools they are supporting to ensure the school's successful performance and growth (Department for Education, 2015). The shift from a supporting role to a leadership model has held profound implications for me in my role as school governor and I now turn to explore how this changing context has shaped my identity.

If we accept the proposal that "people's identities mediate and are mediated by the texts they read, write and talk about" (Moje & Luke, 2009, p. 416) then school governors, constantly participating in these three activities, could develop a strong professional identity. This is particularly so where the texts for consideration come from a variety of sources including government policy, local advice, school data and financial information. The fundamental duty of governors is to read the texts, discuss their implications for the school, and respond by writing strategic plans. The identity of 'governor' forms quickly.

However, this identity is not fixed but fluid, responding to changes over time. While the composition of governing boards has remained relatively stable, the challenges posed by external pressures have necessitated operational changes; "identity…produced, unconsciously, out of embodied practices over time as individuals negotiate shifting structures and fields of power" (Moje & Luke, 2009, p. 418).

Alongside this, the role of school governor has attained a higher profile in England due to increased prominence in the English press. Identity as recognised by others, those that are "not inherent as individuals but brought into being when recognised within a relationship or social context" (Moje & Luke, 2009, p. 419) can reinforce the individual's self-identity as governor.

Theorising of identity is personal and individual, and reading the work of Moje and Luke (2009) has helped me clarify my own pathway. Other EdD students will, and should, use different theories when describing their own identities. Common to all theories is the influence of time: identities "accumulate, merge and thicken over time" (Buss et al., 2014, p. 142). As a Governor for 25 years, and a Chair for 8 years, my textually-based, fluid and socially recognised identity as a strategic school leader was deep and long-established.

PART TWO: TRANSITION

Labaree states that "like any student, [practitioners engaged in doctoral study] are faced with the prospect of learning, and learning means changing into someone different" (Labaree, 2003, p. 21). Specifically, he considers that this can be conceptualised as four shifts in cultural orientation, or worldviews. Entrants into EdD programmes start with and benefit from "a feel for the breadth, depth and complexity of education as an institution that cannot be picked up by reading about it or observing it" (Labaree, 2003, p. 16). Indeed this may be the prospective students' reasoning for their choice to undertake EdDs, as described by Fenge whose "choice of a [Professional Doctorate] over a traditional PhD route, was my perception of myself as a 'practitioner' rather than an 'academic researcher' within the context of my role" (Fenge, 2010, p. 647). My self perception as a strong and experienced practitioner, which on entry to EdD seemed to me to be a source of security, possibly made the "potentially drastic change in the way students look at education and at their work as educationalists" (Labaree, 2003, p. 16) harder for me.

Labaree's four shifts are as follows:

- From normative to analytical
- From personal to intellectual
- From the particular to the universal
- From the experiential to the theoretical

These shifts are in no particular order of chronology or importance: rather they can be used as a framework for the EdD student to consider when mapping their transition to the identity of researcher. As a current student, I cannot claim to have made all four of these shifts: nonetheless, by using the framework to analyse changes in my thinking and practice, I have a clearer idea of where I am and where I need to be. Presented below, is my personal transition: not a typical EdD journey but offered as an example.

From Normative to Analytical: Outcomes to Explanations

Labaree's differentiation here is that education "is a highly normative practice, which focuses on the effort to produce valued outcomes, [whereas] educational research is a distinctly more analytical practice, which focuses on the effort to produce valid explanations" (Labaree, 2003, p. 17). As a governor working within an accountable setting, outcomes had become more important to me, even though I was considering different ways to bring about these outcomes and adjusting my practice accordingly. I needed to make the shift to understanding that the "object of a particular foray into research, as a piece of scholarship, is not to fix a problem of educational practice but to understand more fully the nature of this problem" (Labaree, 2003, p. 17).

Masters' and early doctoral study enabled me to explore leadership literature and improve my own outcome-based practice. Undertaking an EdD can inform the implementation of changes within your own setting, so reading about how "the most efficient executives use a collection of distinct leadership styles – each in the right measure, at just the right time" (Goleman, 2000, p. 78) was exciting and informative. Having analysed my existing style as mainly transactional, and learned that, "transactional dimensions, some of which are considered necessary for successful leadership…are not sufficient [on their own]" (Leithwood & Jantzi, 2009, p. 45), it was appropriate to incorporate elements of transformational leadership, with the aim of "fostering capacity development and higher levels of personal commitment to organizational goals on the part of leaders' colleagues" (ibid.).

This was timely, with the increasing responsibility for school governors necessitating a restructuring of governing boards to devolve some of the workload. Transformational leaders have been defined as "those who seek to radically change an organisation" (Goleman Boyatzis & McKee, 2002, p. 75), and the Governing Body did indeed change significantly during a year of restructuring. New responsibilities were identified with every governor taking on a job description, new committee chairs were elected, and a system of succession planning was devised. The process was complicated and lengthy, with some governors resigning as a result of increased expectations, but those who remained were committed to a new structure that was more sustainable and more effective.

At the time, this seemed to me to be early-stage action research, in its simplest form of "a cyclical activity where you make a plan, carry it through, monitor what goes on, reflect on events critically (using the monitoring data) and move forward" (Lomax, 2007, p. 157). However, looking back, the aim of the exercise was to improve educational practice, not to investigate the nature of the problem. The emphasis was on solutions and outcomes (normative) rather than research (analytical). This was practitioner-thinking, not researcher-thinking.

When beginning to consider the nature of the changes, and the effects of the changes on others, an underlying theme emerged that could not be ignored by a researcher – the ethical element. Not just the ethical considerations to be found in my simplistic view of action research, but something deeper: the long-term effect of "more than just observing protocols…an attitude towards other people and the world" (McNiff, 2013, p. 113) and being "exquisitely sensitive to the impact they are having upon others" (Goleman, 2000, p. 87).

Through this lens, leadership took on a different hue, especially when considering Fullan's warning that "it is easy for authoritative leadership to slip into social engineering when initial excitement cannot be sustained because it cannot be converted to internal commitment" (2001 p. 39). The outcomes-led investigations that I had used to improve practice in my own setting, while research-based, had led to a transitory change, unsustainable because the improvement was only relevant to a certain circumstance.

This indicated the beginnings of a transition to researcher rather than practitioner: the initial shift in thinking, moving away from the self-posed question of "which leadership style will have the most impact in terms of outcomes?" towards a more reflexive consideration of the impact upon others, starting to consider the nature of my practice rather than trying to fix it.

From Personal to Intellectual: Relationships to Ideas

Labaree challenges doctoral students to make the shift to "the primary currency of scholarship, the thing that distinguishes it from other practices in education and gives it value…not relationships but ideas" (Labaree, 2013, p. 19).

Relationships are where "the school system and the governing body system meet" (James et al., 2013a, p. 4), reinforced by governance literature which emphasises the importance of these relationships. Considered of particular importance is the relationship between the head teacher and the chair, which "can be pivotal for the proper functioning of both the school and the governing body" (James et al., 2013b, p. 88). As an avid reader of this literature, my professional identity was shaped by the continuing message.

The characteristic pathway to becoming Chair (election from amongst members of the governing board) indicates the presence of pre-existing positive relationships, whether with other governors or the head teacher: for a Chair to support the relationship-based viewpoint, then, is a "comfortable story" (Kamler & Thomson, 2014, p. 79), a fabrication to support the system that led to their election. My thinking, as a practitioner, was that the relationship-based model that had led to my election as Chair was a suitable model for governance.

This was challenged at a profound level when I was guided towards the ideas of Michel Foucault. As a self-styled practical social scientist, philosophy had previously seemed irrelevant to my stance, but recurrent Foucauldian themes caused me to reconsider my practice.

At an early stage in my doctoral research (and, as so often when you discover a new, favourite author, there is now a comprehensive selection of books by and about Foucault on my bookshelf) my personal theoretical approach is still emerging. As a practitioner, however, two themes resonated deeply:

Panopticism (relationship between governors and school). Foucault's book Discipline and Punish, my first introduction to the philosopher's work, elaborates upon the theme of Bentham's Panopticon (1843). This theoretical building, never actually constructed, took the form of a circular tower with individual illuminated cells around the periphery. A dark central tower may or may not have contained a watcher. Foucault theorised that the invisibility of the central watcher led to an assumption of continual surveillance, whether or not it actually existed: this led to a "guarantee of order" (Foucault, 1975/1977, p. 200). The occupants of the cells always behave as if they are being watched, and conform to the behaviour that is expected from them. The surveillance is therefore "permanent in its effects, even if it is discontinuous in its action" (Foucault, 1975/1977, p. 201).

For me, this prompted the idea of school governors carrying out the work of the Government, who may or may not be watching the school via remote analysis of data. Where previously governors had held a supportive role towards the school, they were now expected to "hold the head teacher to account" (Department for Education, 2015, p. 7), previously a Government duty. Using the Foucauldian metaphor, governors had moved from the position of the watched ones to becoming prominent in the watching. This uncomfortable theory conflicted with my relationship-based thinking as I came to reformulate my position: rather than developing effective relationships with the school, governors could be acting in Panoptic fashion to monitor the implementation of top-down educational policy.

Power (relationship between Chair and governors). The Foucauldian concept of 'power relations', rather than the wider and more common usage of 'power' as a noun, unlocked a different train of thought. Foucault theorised that "Power, with or without a capital letter, which is assumed to exist universally in a concentrated or diffused form, does not exist. Power exists only when it is put into action" (Foucault, 1982, p. 219). The role of Chair, that hitherto had seemed relatively straightforward, took on a different perspective when considered through the lens of "how power is exercised as a tactical and strategical game, exercised from innumerable points, from below, immanently on other relationships, both intentionally and non-subjectively" (Simola, Heikkinen, & Silvonen, 1998, p. 68). I needed to begin to analyse my relationship with other governors. When chairing meetings, was I moving the agenda along in a timely fashion or making decisions about who could participate in the discourse? When trying to recruit new governors, was I filling vacancies with candidates who possessed desirable skills, or seeking out people who shared my truths? As Chair, working in a collegiate group where all members are perceived to be equal, was I creating power by my actions? The answer to this last question, using Foucault's reasoning, was yes.

These are challenging ideas for any practitioner. The long-established stance that a governor was motivated to take up a post in order to contribute to the school, yet has become involved in a power-surveillance framework in which some people may be allowed to contribute but others are excluded, is uncomfortable. On a personal level, my view of relationships was challenged, but my understanding of ideas had expanded. The support/surveillance, relationship/ideas tensions fit the description of "clashing worldviews" (Labaree, 2003, p. 19) that characterise the practitioner-researcher transition. To move forward as a researcher, I had to reconsider my role as a practitioner, as discussed in the next section.

From the Particular to Universal – My School to All Schools

"For educational scholars, the emphasis is on the development of generalities that hold across cases. They usually aim to theorise. This means developing ideas about the way education works that apply to more than one…school" (Labaree, 2003, p. 20). As an experienced Chair, my knowledge of one particular school was extensive. As a Masters' student I had explored other methods of school governance in England and overseas. Combining the two, using ideas of best practice from literature and research, is a powerful tool for improving a practitioner's own setting. Knowledge of one setting, however, while potentially improving practice, is not enough to generate theory. This is a particular issue within education where variations between schools, within a country or between different countries, lead to context-specific practice.

Labaree recognises the difficulty for practitioners as "the uniqueness of their sites of practice also leaves them potentially trapped" (Labaree, 2003, p. 20). As a participant researcher, invigorated by my new understanding of leadership theory but profoundly challenged by the wider picture, it became clear that I had improved my own practice within my own setting as far as I could take it. If I wanted to progress as a researcher, developing theories that could be applied to wider settings, I had to consider resigning as Chair.

Stepping down as Chair of Governors in a school that I had been associated with for twenty years (as parent, part-time teacher, and governor) was a difficult step. James et al., in their study of governance, found that, "The chairs' motivations were grounded in the interests of others and were underpinned by their strong sense of duty. They were somehow morally bound to the role" (2013a, p. 13). This idea certainly resonated with me. I felt a moral obligation to the school. However, the literature discussed in this chapter, and the process of writing the chapter itself, has helped me to navigate through the feeling of guilt – the "how will they manage without me?" thoughts that are probably common to anyone during the resignation process – to a theoretically-based realisation that this was the correct path to follow, both for myself and the Governing Body as a whole.

For the Governing Body, my resignation initiated a positive change. In England, the National Governors' Association (NGA) recommends that "all chairs should normally expect to step down after a maximum of six years in post" (NGA, 2014, para. 6), thereby bringing the position into line with recommendations for good practice in other voluntary sectors. The establishment of succession planning and restructuring that had taken place meant that an appropriately skilled governor was ready to step up.

For me, the metaphor of developing a "theoretical mirror, which [educationalists] can hold up to their own problems of practice in order to see the ways that their problems are both similar to and different from those facing [those] in other settings" (Labaree, 2003, p. 20) is useful here. The implication here is that educational research can be comparative, taking into account one's own setting as well as considering others: the perspective of the familiar, known setting is still important, but the emerging researcher uses it as a base from which to explore other cultures and ideas, rather than focussing on it as a main source.

From Experiential to Theoretical – Self to Social

The example that Labaree gives to illustrate his fourth and final transition spoke directly to me, and made me realise that I still have a long way to go as a researcher and researching professional:

"At any point in the discussion of an academic paper, the student can…introduce an example from his or her own practitioner experience that automatically trumps any claim made by the authors" because "only their experience fits the particulars of their own practice, while also being grounded in their own conception of moral purpose and their own style of personal engagement with [others]" (Labaree, 2003, p. 20). Awareness of my reliance on *my* experiences makes me realise I still need to change my mindset on this issue.

Revisiting Foucault's Panoptic metaphor, the 'watched' have a deep knowledge of their own reality, but this is narrow and restricted, from a fixed perspective. The 'watcher' has a wider, mobile perspective, but even though this allows contextual interpretation of what he observes, he remains at the level of observer only. The professional doctoral student is in the privileged position of being able to move between two different perspectives, with the simultaneous viewpoint of 'watched' and 'watcher', using both deep knowledge and wider interpretation to generate theory.

This transformative journey is enhanced by membership of an EdD/professional doctorate community, where colleagues are drawn from diverse disciplines. All members of the community are drawing on their own practitioner experiences and contexts, but learning from others, as everyone moves from the 'self' of professional reliance to the 'social' of reflective, theoretical-based practices.

PART THREE: 'RESEARCHING PROFESSIONAL' IDENTITY

I did not expect to resign. I did not expect that theory would have such a profound effect upon practice. I did not expect that my reading would have such an impact. It was certainly an unexpected outcome of doctoral study.

This position as a non-Chair, with the "tensions one feels crossing identity boundaries as one moves throughout and across multiple spaces" (Moje & Luke, 2009, p. 431) feels vulnerable and disconcerting: repositioning myself as "just another governor" and letting someone else take the lead, while remaining on the governing body, is unsettling. Revisiting leadership literature was not of much help here: books on leadership recommend ways of encouraging others into leadership, or how to use different leadership styles in times of crisis, but offer little on the planned resignation process, or repositioning of a previous leader in a non-leadership role within the same organisation. More helpful and positive was the idea of using the position of vulnerability as an opportunity to make a significant shift in identity: Fenge, describing her professional doctorate journey, talks of using this "risky territory" (Fenge, 2010, p. 650) as an opportunity to "traverse the space between my practitioner world and doctoral student world" (ibid.).

This position of vulnerability, therefore, is a good place from which to explore and formulate a new identity. While still retaining elements of the identity of 'Chair' (and I still see myself in this category, albeit as a future Chair in a different setting), it allows the opportunity for exploring and formulating a new identity as a researcher.

For a Doctorate of Education student who retains their professional role, what does the researcher/professional identity look like? The two are not mutually exclusive: Labaree considers that the cultural divide, the clashing worldviews referred to earlier in this chapter, should be made explicit to the EdD student as "the value of adopting the researcher perspective – as an addition to rather than replacement for the [educationalist] perspective" (Labaree, 2003, p. 21). There is a certain comfort in this concept that the two can co-exist, that the professional identity does not have to be left behind.

In the study *Developing researching professionals in an EdD program: From learners and leaders to scholarly and influential practitioners*, Buss et al. suggest a different model with three different identities for Doctorate of Education (EdD) students, those of "learners, leaders and action researchers" (2014, p. 137). Their research indicates that students have all three of these multiple identities at the beginning and at the end of their EdDs: however, there is a shift in the balance of the three identities as the EdD progresses (with the learner and leader identities being strongest at the beginning of the programme, and the researcher identity at the end).

They suggest that doctoral study involves a gradual synthesis of the three identities as the study progresses, to foster "the construction of a researching professional identity status" (ibid.). The status is defined as that of Scholarly and Influential Practitioners, recognising the professionally-based route that the practitioner has taken to become a researcher. There is an acknowledgment of the practitioner status that Doctorate of Education students bring to their research, and a reminder that the practitioner status will exist after the research is finished, in the comment that "integrating practical and research knowledge that links theory and enquiry develops habits of mind that are beneficial to program participants during the program and long after it through their professional careers" (Buss et al., 2014, p. 157). For me, at this stage in my Doctorate in Education, the status and definition of Scholarly and Influential Practitioner makes sense, and is something to aim for as I begin to integrate the three identities.

CLOSING REFLECTIONS

Practitioner or researcher? Or something else, a scholarly and influential practitioner that is the researching professional? This chapter invites those who are considering or undertaking a professional doctorate to consider whether there is a continuum between the two and, if so, where they place themselves along it. Those who choose the professional doctorate route are likely to start with a strong professional identity, which can help or hinder the transition. By exploring two different models of identity (Labaree: education practitioner and researching professional and Buss et al.: learner, leader and researcher), the reader may discover, as I did, that professional identity is not lost: rather, it is enhanced.

REFERENCES

Bacon, W. (1978). *Public accountability and the schooling system: A sociology of school board democracy.* London: Harper and Row.

Buss, R., Zambo, R., Zambo, D., & Williams, T. (2014). Developing researching professionals in an EdD program: From learners and leaders to scholarly and influential practitioners. *Higher Education, Skills and Work-based Learning, 4*(2), 137–160.

Department for Education. (2015). *Governance handbook for trustees of academies and multi-academy trusts and governors of maintained schools.* London: Department for Education.

Fenge, L. (2010). Sense and sensibility: Making sense of a professional doctorate. *Reflective Practice, 11*(5), 645–656.

Foucault, M. (1977). *Discipline and punish: The birth of the prison* (A. Sheridan, Trans.). London: Penguin. (Original work published 1975).

Foucault, M. (1982). The subject and power. In H. Dreyfus & P. Rabinow (Eds.), *Michel Foucault: Beyond structuralism and hermeneutics.* Brighton: The Harvester Press.

Fullan, M. (2001). *Leading in a culture of change.* San Francisco, CA: Jossey-Bass.

Goleman, D. (2000). Leadership that gets results. *Harvard Business Review, 78*(2), 78–90.

Goleman, D., Boyatzis, R., & McKee, A. (2002). *The new leaders: Transforming the art of leadership into the science of results.* London: Sphere.

James, C., Brammer, S., Connolly, M., Spicer, D., James, J., & Jones, J. (2013a). *The chair of the school governing body in England: Roles, relationships and responsibilities.* Reading: CfBT Education Trust.

James, C., Brammer, S., Connolly, M., Spicer, D., James, J., & Jones, J. (2013b). The challenges facing school governing bodies in England: A 'perfect storm'? *Management in Education, 27*(3), 84–90.

Kamler, B., & Thomson, P. (2006/2014). *Helping doctoral students write: Pedagogies for supervision* (2nd ed.). London: Routledge.

Labaree, D. (2003). The peculiar problem of preparing educational researchers. *Educational Researcher, 32*(4), 13–22.

Leithwood, K., & Jantzi, D. (2009). Transformational leadership. In B. Davies (Ed.), *The essentials of school leadership* (2nd ed.). London: Sage.

Lomax, P. (2007). Action research. In A. Briggs & M. Coleman (Eds.), *Research methods in educational leadership and management* (pp. 156–172). London: Sage.

McNiff, J. (2013). *Action research: Principles and practice* (3rd ed.). Abingdon: Routledge.

Moje, E., & Luke, A. (2009). Literacy and identity: Examining the metaphors in history and contemporary research. *Reading Research Quarterly, 44*(4), 415–437.

National Governors' Association. (2014). *Governance* [online]. Retrieved February 6, 2016, from http://www.nga.org.uk/About-Us/Campaigning/Policies/Governance.aspx

Simola, H., Heikkinen, S., & Silvonen, J. (1998). A catalog of possibilities: Foucaultian history of truth and education research. In T. Popkewitz & M. Brennan (Eds.), *Foucault's challenge: Discourse, knowledge and power in education* (pp. 64–90). New York, NY: Teachers College Press.

PART 3

GENERATING IMPACT

JULIA FLUTTER

9. CONSTRUCTING IMPACT

INTRODUCTION

The preceding chapters have drawn on professional doctorate students and staff members' narratives, and this one will also begin with an account of a personal research voyage which will be used to illustrate differing constructions of impact. As will become apparent, the notions of impact proposed are shaped by the waters I have travelled through as a researcher in education. This narrative is based on a Keynote Presentation which I presented for the annual EdD One-Day-Conference at the University of Cambridge's Faculty of Education in June 2015. This led to an invitation to contribute to this book. The presentation, entitled '*Ripples on the surface or making a splash? What happens when educational research goes out into the big, wide, world?*' focused on the varied forms and levels of impact I have experienced during my research career and distinguished two, distinct kinds of impact, identified through the metaphors of 'ripples' and 'splashes'. Impact ripples are subtle and small-scale, moving away from the source of movement over time and space to effect change on their surroundings. Impact splashes, by contrast, are designed to produce an immediate, transformative effect and these are aimed for and planned from an early stage in the research process. The waves from the 'splash' impact may be contained within the original site or travel further, as in the case of the Cambridge Primary Review, a large-scale, longitudinal inquiry on the condition of primary (elementary) education, discussed later in this chapter.

A RESEARCHER'S TALE – MAKING YOUR WAY

My own research journey began with postgraduate studies at the University of Cambridge's School of Education (now the Faculty of Education) in the early 1990s when I enrolled on the Education and Psychological course studying young children's psychological development. My research was focused on an area of enquiry which fascinated me, personally and professionally, having previously worked in nursery education where I had become aware of the centrality of talk in the development of children's thinking and learning. At the end of my studies I took up a post as Research Assistant on a four year, longitudinal project called *Making Your Way Through Secondary School*, led by Professor Jean Rudduck at Homerton College, Cambridge. This ambitious, ground-breaking study was the first in a series of research investigations I was involved with Jean Rudduck which set out to

P. Burnard et al. (Eds.), Transformative Doctoral Research Practices for Professionals, 115–125.

explore students' perspectives of teaching and learning and which later became part of the foundations underpinning the development of 'student voice' as a movement in education (Rudduck & McIntyre, 2007). Surprisingly perhaps, few educational research projects had previously considered investigating what students have to say about their experiences as learners: although students' views had been recorded as sources of data in some psychological and social studies, their views had rarely been taken into account as 'expert witnesses' for educational research and practice.

Making Your Way's findings revealed a complex and fascinating picture of the factors that influenced students' learning and attainment in school. At the time England had introduced a National Curriculum for the first time and educational policy had begun to enter a phase of marketization where schools were to compete for student enrolments. Viewed from the students' perspectives, the impact of these changes was profoundly unsettling and not wholly beneficial to their learning and identities as learners. Our project's evidence clearly showed how the interplay between policy and practice impinged on students' levels of motivation and engagement and it was through detailed, sustained analysis of our data that were able to identify some key factors and moments affecting the trajectories of students' school careers. In the first years of secondary school, for example, we noted how some students became disengaged with the learning process. Students told us that they regarded these early years as being unimportant and the 'serious years', when they would need to work hard to have examination success, lay far ahead. For some students, this drift away from learning at this early stage would have lasting consequences when they were unable to make up for lost ground in their learning later on. Unable to catch up with their peers, these students drifted away from schooling and many left compulsory education without the qualifications they would need to take up further education or qualified employment.

Another important aspect to our findings lay with the process of student consultation itself and the way in which the students had responded to these learning-focused dialogues with adults. We were struck by the serious, considered comments they made about their experiences as learners and our data brought to light students' misconceptions and misunderstandings which teachers had largely been unaware of. Although initially teachers had been concerned that students would be critical or disrespectful in their comments about the quality of teaching, they too found the students' views constructive and insightful. As a result of their involvement in the project the schools had begun to explore the potential benefits of student consultation as a means of developing new directions for school improvement and they were keen to extend this approach after the project finished. The first, significant ripples of impact were therefore felt by the students, teachers and researchers who were immediately involved and subsequently moved outwards into the schools where the project took place.

On a broader level, the wider *ripples of impact* continued to spread outwards as the project's findings began to raise fundamental questions about the ways in which young people are regarded in society at large as well as within the educational system itself. We observed that many young people experience autonomy and empowerment in their lives outside school and yet schools offered few opportunities for students to take responsibility or have an active role in school decision-making. These findings led us to recommend that the structure of schools should be changed to embrace the notion of schools as communities of learning based on values of respect, responsibility and autonomy (Rudduck, Wallace, & Chaplain, 1996). This recommendation chimes with Article 12 of the United Nations Convention on the Rights of the Child (UNCRC) (1989) which states that:

> States Parties shall assure to the child who is capable of forming his or her own views the right to express those views freely in all matters affecting the child, the views of the child being given due weight in accordance with the age and maturity of the child. (UNCRC, 1989, p. 3)

Making Your Way Through Secondary School helped to instigate a new line of research and its approach and conclusions have continued to resonate in educational policymaking and practice across many countries and all phases of education, from nursery provision through to postgraduate study. Its widest ripples have travelled over twenty years in diverse and often surprising directions (cf. Rudduck & McIntyre, 2007). But it is important to acknowledge that its *impact* has also had limitations and constraints that would be familiar to researchers in working in other subjects, professions and contexts. The institutional constraints of the schools we were working with meant that we were often unable to effect the changes that students wanted. As visiting researchers, it was not within our power or remit to bring about such direct and immediate change and, although students were given access to our findings, there was a sense in which the students remained 'sources of data' rather than active agents.

IMPACT RIPPLES – THE STUDENT VOICE MOVEMENT

The projects which built on the legacy of *Making Your Way* included the Economic and Social Research Council's Teaching and Learning Research Programme's Network Project, 'Consulting Pupils About Teaching and Learning' which was, sadly, to be Jean Rudduck's final, large-scale research study with her untimely death in 2007. The Network project marked the 10 year point in our student voice research and in addition to working with schools, it enabled us to look beyond the school system to consider the changing constructions of children and childhood which underpinned the principles of the student voice movement in society at large. We found evidence in this project that student voice principles were beginning to lead to change more widely in the UK (Rudduck & Flutter, 2007). Together with other influences such as the UNCRC (above), student voice principles had begun to challenge traditional views of children and young people as being incapable and dependent and were opening up new understandings of their capabilities. Amongst the new arenas where the voices of children and young people were to be heard were courts of law, local government youth councils, and even the Houses of Parliament with the introduction of the Youth Parliament. But the ripples were to continue to spread beyond the shores of the UK.

In 2009, Alison Cook-Sather (Byrn Mawr College, Pennsylvania) became the Jean Rudduck Visiting Fellow and the first in a series of international seminars was held at the Faculty of Education in Cambridge. Under Alison's energetic leadership, researchers, policymakers, school and university students and educational practitioners from around the world came together to exchange ideas and experiences of student voice research and practices. Countries represented included Australia, Canada, Chile, Denmark, Italy, Lebanon, New Zealand, Northern Ireland, Sweden, the UK and the USA. The seminars enabled us to look closely at the ever-widening range of different principles and practices which characterize student voice within different contexts and cultures: excitingly, our ripples of impact were finally beginning to come together to form greater waves of transformative change across the world.

One of the most interesting themes to emerge in these seminar discussions has been the unexpectedly varied ways in which the concept of 'student voice' is understood and enacted in different countries, reflecting their particular social, political and cultural contexts and agendas. Whilst in some countries, like the UK, student voice has become focused on pedagogical aims (Rudduck & McIntyre, 2007), in others, like Sweden and Chile, it is seen as an essential foundation for democratic participation. As *ripples of impact* travel further from their origin they can change in form and the ways in which they shape the landscapes they encounter become increasingly unpredictable.

When I began working with Jean Rudduck in 1994, the term 'student voice' was virtually unknown and if used as a key word in literature searching, the results would have referred largely to medical papers on vocal chords. The same keyword search performed today would produce thousands of books, articles and conference papers describing the myriad directions student voice research, policy and practice has taken across the world's stage. However, when I reflect on my career in student voice research my attention does not focus on this worldwide expansion because it overlooks the most important impact of this work for me personally. The *ripples* that start the journey, and which I feel most keenly, are those I have encountered when working with individual head teachers (or school principals, teachers, school advisers, students and schools). The moments in my career that I look back on with greatest pleasure and the strongest sense of achievement are those occasions when a teacher or a student has spoken of the difference that listening, or being listening to, can make.

At a personal level, the student voice voyage has been immensely exciting but there also remains a sense of frustration that the ripples of impact continue to fall against stony ground in many ways. Partly this is explained perhaps by the many competing pressures that governments, schools, teachers and learners are under but

I believe it also reflects a deep-seated reluctance to challenge our assumptions about children and young people, and the relationship between teacher and learner.

> In answer to our original question – what's in it for schools? – we would suggest that the pupil voice offers a different path for the future development of education. The growth of interest in listening to what young people have to say, both within schools and outside, bodes well perhaps but we must be wary of the 'bandwagon' appeal…that can turn a new development into a short-lived 'flavour of the month'. The transformative potential of pupil participation will be lost if established structures within schools prevent this movement from taking root and flourishing. There is clear evidence that the political and social climate has begun to warm to the principle of involving children and young people but we must wait to see whether schools will provide the right conditions for pupil voice to grow. (Flutter & Rudduck, 2004, pp. 138–139)

However, the student voice voyage continues and the next stage in my own story leads into new waters where *splashes of impact* come to the fore with the experiences of the Cambridge Primary Review.

'SPLASH' IMPACT – THE CAMBRIDGE PRIMARY REVIEW

In 2007 my research career took a different turn when I took up the post of Research Associate for the Cambridge Primary Review, a large-scale research project (funded by the Esmée Fairbairn Foundation) which had been recently established at the Faculty of Education in Cambridge. This new role brought my engagement in student voice into a completely new research frame and, unlike my work with Jean Rudduck, this project adopted an ambitious, high-profile remit which was designed to create immediate impact splashes from its point of its inception in 2006. The Review's agenda sought to examine and evaluate primary (elementary) education in England on a holistic, national scale for the first time in over 40 years (see below).

1. With respect to public provision in England, the Review will seek to identify the purposes which the primary phase of education should serve, the values which it should espouse, the curriculum and learning environment which it should provide, and the conditions which are necessary in order to ensure both that these are of the highest and most consistent quality possible, and that they address the needs of children and society over the coming decades.
2. The Review will pay close regard to national and international evidence from research, inspection and other sources on the character and adequacy of current provision in respect of the above, on the prospects for recent initiatives, and on other available options. It will seek the advice of expert advisers and witnesses, and it will invite submissions and take soundings

> from a wide range of interested agencies and individuals, both statutory and non-statutory.
> 3. The Review will publish both interim findings and a final report. The latter will combine evidence, analysis and conclusions together with recommendations for both national policy and the work of schools and other relevant agencies.
>
> *Remit of The Cambridge Primary Review (Alexander, 2010)*

Evidence for the Review was to be drawn from a range of sources including analysis of official policy, commissioned reviews of published, national and international research, consultations and submissions from all those involved in the lives and education of English, primary school aged children, including the children themselves, their teachers and parents, organisations and communities. Analysis of these various strands of data allowed the Project Team, led by Professor Robin Alexander, to construct a comprehensive and richly detailed picture of children's lives and education in England during this time period and the evidence was subsequently used to construct a wide-ranging set of recommendations for improving policy and practice (Alexander, 2010).

From an early stage, the Review began to release initial findings from its work with the intention of creating a public discourse about the issues it was investigating and a series of interim reports were made freely available online and in print. In addition, the Review engaged directly with the media which raised its profile within the public domain and resulted in its interim reports making headlines in the UK's national newspapers on several occasions throughout 2007–2009 and the publication of its Final Report in October 2009 created a storm of press attention around the world. The immediacy of the impact splash was intentional, but the responses and outcomes were beyond the Review's control and were not wholly positive. Robin Alexander, the Review's Director (and now Chair of the Cambridge Primary Review Trust) takes up the story:

> We published our six interim reports, together with briefings and press releases, in two instalments. As might be expected, our research teams exposed the complexity of the data and the difficulty of making hard and fast judgements, especially about trends over time. We identified evidence of initial success but also problems. Acting on the well-known journalistic maxim 'First simplify, then exaggerate', the press ignored the positives in our reports and amplified the negatives with baleful headlines like: 'Primary tests blasted by experts' ... 'Too much testing harms primary school pupils' ... 'Literacy drive has almost no impact' ... 'Millions wasted on teaching reading' ... 'An oppressive system that is failing our children' ... 'School system test-obsessed' ... 'England's children among the most tested' ... 'Our children are tested to destruction' ... 'Primary pupils let down by Labour' ... 'Primary schools have got worse' and 'A shattering failure for our masters'. (Alexander, 2014, p. 9)

The Government response to such provocative coverage was predictably hostile, with official statements and Government ministers issuing rebuttals and critical accusations about the Review's credibility. It was evident, however, that these official statements were directed at the image of the Review's message as portrayed in the Press rather than the Review's actual evidence and vision. Nonetheless, as one national newspaper journalist pointed out, the damage was done:

Since 2003, every education secretary and minister has been distinguished by an almost wilful determination to ignore the mass of research that does not suit their agenda. Politically, that is the easiest choice. They are encouraged in this by their senior civil servants, whose careers have been built around delivering a particular agenda, and who have nothing to gain by seeing it change course. What is truly alarming is that ministers rarely even glimpse the reports they dismiss. Last year I mentioned a particularly critical Ofsted report to one minister. 'Oh, my people tell me there's nothing new in that,' he said, breezily. In fact, it had a great deal that was new and important, and the individuals who put thousands of man-hours into preparing it were probably writing it for an audience of three – of which the minister who never read it was the most important one. It seems that the Cambridge Primary Review is meeting the same fate. This extensive, diligent review of published evidence and new research was dismissed in 10 seconds by another minister in a private conversation: 'My people say it's rehashed.' Publicly, the Department for Children, Schools and Families has written off the latest reports as 'recycled, partial and out-of-date'. (Russell, *The Guardian,* 2008)

However, whilst acknowledging the drawbacks to the Review's strategy for generating this form of impact, Robin Alexander points out it brought the interim reports into the frame of public attention and discussion, and thus they had achieved their aim for stimulating public discourse about primary aged children's lives and education:

In one sense the strategy was highly successful: on five of the ten occasions between 2007 and 2009 when the Review published its reports, independent media analysis showed that it was top UK news story overall. What we couldn't control, of course, was the nature of that media coverage. (Alexander, 2014, p. 11)

Of course, the Review's *splash impact* goes far beyond the official responses to its Press coverage and since the Final Report was published, it has established a network for primary schools interested in developing practice in accordance with the Review's findings, recommendations and principles. In 2010, the Cambridge Primary Review Trust came into being, a not-for-profit company partnered initially by international education publisher, Pearson Education. The Trust's mission is to:

Continue to address the themes, questions, priorities and challenges that lie at the heart of CPR's mission to maximise the quality of young children's primary education.

Help schools and teachers to build institutional, individual and collective capacity to respond effectively yet discriminatingly to the requirements of policy, but also to address those important aspects of professional practice and larger educational questions with which policy does not deal.

Continue the task of national and international dissemination and discussion of CPR's evidence, ideas and principles, using a variety of print, broadcast and online media.

Revisit and where necessary extend the Cambridge Primary Review's evidence base in relation to the above.

Continue to engage with and seek to influence government, opposition, professional associations and other key national stakeholders in pursuit of a generous and relevant vision of primary education grounded in evidence and achieved through sound policy and practice.

Review, consolidate and extend the Cambridge Primary Review's professional network, its databases and its regional centres.

Organise at appropriate intervals a major international conference to foreground evidence and issues germane to the advancement of high quality primary education and to showcase the work of the Trust, its partners and others sharing its vision. (Cambridge Primary Review Trust website: www.cprtrust.org.uk accessed 22.4.2016)

In addition to the media and work with influencing practitioners, the Review also sought to inform policymakers' thinking via face-to-face meetings with government ministers, Department of Education officials and opposition parties and it has presented formal submissions to government public reviews on assessment, school inspection, professional teacher standards and the curriculum. The Review's success in securing public attention led the government to respond by launching its own review of primary education with a more limited remit called the Independent Review of the Primary Curriculum (which became known in the media as 'The Rose Review' because it was directed by Sir Jim Rose). The Rose Review recommendations on the primary curriculum were published shortly before the Cambridge Primary Review's final report and were to be implemented in schools in the next school year. However, following the general election a few months later and a change of government, the Rose Review's outcomes were shelved and the new Coalition Government replaced them with its own proposals.

Adopting such a strategy for creating direct, transformative impact sets the Cambridge Primary Review apart from many other educational research projects and its balance of practice-based and academic evidence parallels, to some extent, the principle of professional doctoral research which also combines these evidential sources. The Review's mission to support the development of educational policy and practice, and to provide a framework for discussion and improvement, remains a work-in-progress but there are indications that its efforts have resulted in significant strides forward contributing not only to the English system but also to educational practices and policymaking in other countries around the world (REF, 2014).

CONSTRUCTING IMPACT

Throughout this chapter the thematic motifs of *ripples* and *splashes of impact* have been explored, illustrated through narrative examples drawn from my own career as a professional researcher in education, and now we turn to consider how these metaphors of impact intersect with professional doctoral research, beginning with impact 'ripples'. We have seen how impact ripples are characterized by their low profile and small scale; they emanate from their origin relatively slowly and organically, spreading gradually outwards and effecting change. The energy which drives these *impact ripples* comes from within the professional doctoral student and its most immediate effects will be noticed in changes to the student's professional and personal identity. In contrast with impact ripples, the *'splash'* impact metaphor denotes impact that is directed at specific outcomes, is often high-profile and large-scale, and seeks immediate, transformative effect, as exemplified in the example of the Cambridge Primary Review. We will return to consider this type of impact later on.

As we noted earlier, one of the most important and innovative dimensions of professional doctorates lies in their potential for generating *impact ripples* which extend directly from the centre Burgess, Weller and Wellington (2011) categorised the impact of professional doctorates as being tripartite with (i) impact on personal lives, (ii) impact on professional careers and (iii) impact on professional discourse. Focusing on the identity aspect of impact Scott and Morrison (2010) note that this process of change is fluid and complex and often gives rise to tensions and compartmentalization in a student's life:

> Professional doctorates…with their weak boundaries between disciplinary and practicum knowledge, may create different forms of identity in the student. Yet, what is significant is that even in professional doctorates the discipline retains a more powerful hold for many students than the profession. During the various rites of passage from competent professional, to novice doctoral initiate, through to finally achieving doctoral status at the convocation ceremony, 'schizophrenic' tendencies are averted for students by the compartmentalisation of identities whilst at university and in professional employment – one being 'academic' and the other 'professional'. (Scott & Morrison, 2010, p. 25)

As we have seen in many of the narratives included in this book, becoming a professional doctoral student is often experienced as a life-changing moment with profound consequences.

Velencei et al. (2015) focus on the outer ellipses of *impact ripples* where intersection with impact ripples from other sources begins. They argue that professional doctoral research, particularly where it creates spaces for transdisciplinary research communities to arise, has a capacity for finding solutions to problems that are '…felt locally, thought about globally' and therefore '…with locating solution[s] that potentially have global impact' (2015, p. 2770). However, for some academics the professional doctorate's problem-solving capacity represents an uncomfortable step away from long-established, academic forms of 'pure' knowledge construction and could even threaten existing knowledge structures in higher education institutions (Scott & Morrison, 2010). This concern stems perhaps from an unwillingness to challenge the hegemony of such institutional structures and risks a loss of opportunities for alternative models of knowledge creation.

However, the *splash impact* of professional doctoral research – that is to say, its intentional, transformative power – may lie in its potential to disrupt long-established, stagnant knowledge domains which serve to constrain problem-solving and innovation. Professional doctoral research represents an alternative way of constructing and creating knowledge through its capacity to entwine two strands of knowledge creation in equal measure: one derived from professional experience and expertise, and the other derived through theoretical, academic discourse. Working these two strands together lends tensile strength to the threads of understanding essential for tackling the problems we face at local, national and global levels.

CONCLUDING COMMENTS

The story of student voice illustrates how slowly the *impact ripples* can travel and how difficult it can be to anticipate, steer or even know which directions they will travel in. Once the ripples leave the researcher's control in the ocean, they can fall against resistant cliffs or merge with others to become greater waves of change. As researchers and professionals we need to accept that sometimes we can do no more than light the 'slow fuse of possibility' (Fielding, 1997). The Keynote Presentation at the EdD conference introduced the students to these two ways of thinking about impact with the intention of illustrating what forms impact can take and the reasons why researchers need to be both aware and wary of how these ripples and splashes effect changes that are both within and beyond the researcher's control.

In the chapters which follow, professional doctorate student, Rebecca Kitchen (Chapter 10) and doctorate educator, Riikka Hofmann (Chapter 11) share their own, individual experiences of research impact. Whilst each account in Part 3 is distinctive and unique, discernible themes emerge, allowing us to begin to forge understandings at a deeper, theoretical level regarding the value and potential for transformative impact of professional doctoral research.

REFERENCES

Alexander, R. (Ed.). (2010). *Children, their world, their education: Final report and recommendations of the Cambridge Primary Review*. London: Routledge.

Alexander, R. (2014, May 13). *Evidence, policy and the reform of primary education: A cautionary tale.* The 2014 Godfrey Thomson Trust Lecture, University of Edinburgh, Edinburgh.

Burgess, H., Weller, G., & Wellington, J. (2011). Tensions in the purpose and impact of professional doctorates. *Work-Based Learning e-Journal, 2*(1), 1–20.

Fielding, M. (1997). Beyond school effectiveness and school improvement: Lighting the slow fuse of possibility. *Curriculum Journal, 8*(1), 7–37.

Flutter, J., & Rudduck, J. (2004). *Consulting pupils- what's in it for schools?* London: Routledge Falmer.

Research Excellence Framework. (2014). *REF 2014 impact case study REF3b*. Retrieved April 28, 2016, from http://impact.ref.ac.uk/casestudies2/refservice.svc/GetCaseStudyPDF/19618

Rudduck, J., & McIntyre, D. (2007). *Improving learning through consulting pupils*. London: Taylor and Francis.

Rudduck, J., Wallace, G., & Chaplain, R. (1996). *School improvement: What can pupils tell us?* London: David Fulton.

Russell, J. (2008, March 26). The NUT has cried wolf too often, but this time it's right. *The Guardian.*

Scott, D., & Morrison, M. (2010). New sites and agents for research education in the United Kingdom: Making and taking doctoral identities. *Work-Based Learning e-Journal, 1*(1), 15–34.

Velencei, J., Baracskai, Z., & Dörfler, V. (2015, July 6–8). *Educating the transdisciplinary mind: Curriculum design for a professional doctorate*. Proceedings of the EDULEARN15 Conference, Barcelona, Spain.

REBECCA KITCHEN

10. WHOSE STONE IS IT ANYWAY? ARTICULATING THE IMPACT OF EXPLORATORY DOCTORAL RESEARCH FOR PROFESSIONAL EDUCATORS

INTRODUCTION

The process of research can be likened to that of throwing a stone into a pond. Firstly, a single stone is selected from the many that lie on the bank; not so big that it is unmanageable and not so small that it lacks impetus. The thrower launches the stone having considered the force of the throw, its direction and subsequent trajectory. It hits the water in the pond sending up splashes, radiating ripples or, if the thrower is particularly unlucky or has not thought enough about the stone selection or trajectory, the stone sinks without trace. So it is with research. The researcher carefully chooses their research topic – their stone – and plans its trajectory, the research approach and methodology. As the completed thesis hits the research community into which it has been thrown, so it creates impact as a dramatic splash or as ripples that slowly permeate practice and policy.

In reality, professional doctoral research is not as straightforward as this metaphor would suggest. Many research projects, rather than being an individual endeavour, are shaped by the stakeholders that invest in them. Government policy, institutional constraints and colleagues can cause research to be pulled in different directions to respond to multiple and often conflicting interests. However, whilst these multiple interests affect the trajectory of the impact of research, they also have the potential to make the ripples of its impact travel further. More people are invested in the outcomes and so it is in their interest for there to be ripples that permeate practice and policy.

So, whose stone is it anyway? Whilst the professional doctoral researcher may have more control over the choice of the research topic itself, in some respects they may lack full control of its trajectory, influence and impact. They have some responsibility to ensure that, through dissemination, the ripples of impact reach out and shape change for those who have a vested interest in its outcomes. Yet, the perceived lack of control over the research may delimit or even hinder the impact of the research within the context in which it was conceived. This chapter presents the narrative of my own research story to illustrate how a consideration of questions around impact and identity can be used to navigate through the professional doctoral

P. Burnard et al. (Eds.), Transformative Doctoral Research Practices for Professionals, 127–139.

journey and highlight the fluidity and reflexivity which can enrich it. By deploying and critiquing the metaphor of the research stone it considers the following questions:

- Why did I pick up the stone? (or, why did I choose to engage in professional doctoral research and how and why did I select my research topic?)
- How has throwing the stone impacted upon me as the thrower? (or, how has engaging in professional doctoral research impacted upon my professional identity?)
- What ripples does my stone have the potential to make? (or, what are the wider impacts of carrying out professional doctoral research such as this?)

NARRATIVE

Why Did I Pick Up the Stone? (or, Why Did I Choose to Engage in Professional Doctoral Research and How and Why Did I Select My Research Topic?)

Picking up a stone is a conscious and deliberate action and so one might assume that the answer to this question is fairly straightforward. However, in reality, it has taken the writing of this chapter to make sense of my motivations for engaging in doctoral study and the decision to journey down the path of a professional Doctorate of Education (EdD) rather than a Doctorate of Philosophy (PhD)[1] (Weick, 1995). As Kenway and McLeod (2004) highlight, the experience has allowed the time and space to construct my own identity as a practitioner researcher self-consciously and reflexively.

Why did I choose to engage in professional doctoral research? Whilst it may appear self-indulgent and almost confessional to go back and describe my life over the last eight years, arguably this critical reflection is required in order for the reader to fully understand my motivations, and to be fully transparent (Van Maanen, 1988). Indeed, Wellington and Sikes (2006) find that biography is essential in determining the motivation and impact of those engaging in a professional doctorate. In 2008, the school where I was Curriculum Manager for Humanities and Head of Geography became a 'Training School', an English government designation which attracted funding for initiatives to improve teaching and learning. There were fortnightly 'Learning Lunches' where staff would deliver and attend workshops to share good practice, and approximately 20% of staff, including myself, completed Teacher Learning Academy (TLA) projects at stage 1 and 2 (College of Teachers, 2013). The Training School initiative which had the greatest impact on my professional development, however, was a collaboration where the school was used as a hub and lecturers from Oxford Brookes University would travel to deliver sessions leading to an MA in Education.

At the first of these Masters sessions I had an epiphany and knew that I had found my niche. I had always been a good geographer but had never been an excellent one (grade B at A level and a rejection from the University of Cambridge were two enduring memories from my Sixth Form experience) and I knew that I was a good teacher (but again, probably not an excellent one). It was the fusion of the two that inspired me. I quickly found that I could take the theory that was being discussed and apply it to my practical classroom experience and vice versa. I thrived on the sessions where I could contribute to discussion and when it came to writing assignments had the feeling of being a student again, of scholarship. I would go to the university library and take several hours out of my hectic life. It made me reminisce about my days as an undergraduate and it made me realise how much I had missed and how much I enjoy writing.

In my third year, in between teaching, taking my two young sons to karate and tennis lessons and everything else that working mothers have to organise, I wrote my dissertation "What is geography?: How do Year 7 perceptions of geography change as a result of teaching?". Roberts (2010) argues that the research which is of most practical use to teachers is that which is conducted by teachers themselves: the sense of achievement as I completed each chapter and the demonstrable and positive impact that the research, and my thinking around the research, was having in the classroom was transformative. I was also incredibly fortunate to have a friendly, wise and experienced supervisor who challenged me, supported me and subsequently documented my experiences (Catling, 2015).

Whilst the tangible outcome of a Masters study is the dissertation and, more often than not, supervision is focused on the negotiation of this written product, Green and Lee (1995) and Petersen (2007) argue that what is also going on is the negotiation of identity. In this case, my supervisor was instrumental in helping to shape my identity as a researcher; I was, as Lave and Wenger (1991) suggest, at the start of the process of becoming. He encouraged me to write journal articles based on my findings and assumed that I would take my research journey further, that a doctorate was the next natural step (Kitchen, 2013a, 2013b). It would certainly fill the looming dissertation void which, as Herman highlights, is "an emotional endeavour seldom mentioned in the research literature" (2010, p. 290).

In terms of those who choose to engage in a professional doctorate, Wellington and Sikes (2006) and Scott et al. (2004) identify three groups: those at the beginning of their careers who feel the need to be 'initiated' into their chosen professions, those some way into their careers who see the doctorate as career enhancement and those who undertake the qualification for personal development and intellectual challenge. I very much straddled the latter two categories. I did not want promotion but I wanted to add breadth to my career and also to challenge myself intellectually, motivations which Wellington (2010) identifies as intrinsic and personal.

How and why did I select my research topic? Having decided to engage in a professional doctorate I then needed to pick up the stone, to select a research topic which both interested me and was worth investigation (Brown, 2010). Satisfying my interests was fairly straightforward. I had discovered, through engaging in Masters research, that, generally, it was Geography Education Research (GER) and more specifically exploring students perceptions of the subject that I was interested in. The actual focus of the research topic, however, came from a direction that I had not expected. I had just taken eight months off on maternity leave and, on returning to my classroom, I noticed the proportion of ethnic minority students in my Key Stage 3^2 classes appeared significantly higher than previously. Not only this: the ethnic minority students in my Key Stage 4^3 and Key Stage 5^4 classes, where geography is optional, were conspicuous by their absence.

At first I wondered whether this was an actual increase or something that I had simply noticed on my return. However, student data held by the school showed that in 2005, 16% of the school was non-White British and this figure had increased to 25% by 2013. Furthermore, the most dramatic increase, from 19% to 24%, occurred between 2011 and 2012, the year of my maternity leave. During the period 2005 to 2013, the proportion of ethnic minority students (that is to say, those identifying as not White British) opting for geography increased but not by the same rate: in 2005, 8% of students from an ethnic minority opted to take GCSE or A level geography; this rose to 14% by 2013. Research by Vidal Rodeiro (2009), Weeden (2011) and Singleton (2012) at GCSE level and Vidal Rodeiro (2009) at A level suggested a similar picture nationally: ethnic minority students are under-represented compared to their White British counterparts in the study of GCSE and A level Geography.

For my doctoral research, therefore, I decided to explore ethnic minority students' perceptions of geographical knowledge and the influences which shape their perceptions. The research design is structured on a multiple case basis with a sample of eight individual cases, all of whom are high-achieving girls (my school is a single sex grammar school in the South-East of England). Data gathering is largely qualitative and includes diverse types of data: collages, critical incident charting and semi-structured interviews investigating students' perceptions of geographical knowledge and subject choices at both GCSE and A level.

I had found my stone and yet, the more I read, the more was I acutely aware of its power but also of its potential for possibly causing damage. Weeden (2006) suggests that exploring ethnic minority student perspectives is a potentially rich and important vein of research and yet, within the field of geography education, this is limited to the work of Bar-Gal and Sofer (2010) working within an Israeli context. Exploring student perspectives of geographical knowledge, the stories that relate to these perspectives and how students account for their option choices at GCSE and A level within a UK context therefore appears both to contain the potential to shape new knowledge and to be, both in a pragmatic sense and morally, worthwhile (Brown, 2010; Wagner, 2010). However, it is critical to understand that this research does not seek to change ethnic minority perceptions of geographical knowledge. Even suggesting this implies that their perspective is somehow wrong and that I have the power to allow my definition of reality to prevail over theirs (John, 2003, p. 47). Rather, its intention is to challenge the notion of a single ethnic story and to shine a light on the voices of students who might otherwise not be heard or valued (Adichie, 2009; Biddulph, 2011).

How Has Throwing the Stone Impacted Upon Me as the Thrower? (or, How Has Engaging in Professional Doctoral Research Impacted Upon My Professional Identity?)

As I noted in the previous section, I became aware of my changing identity as a researcher, yet I embarked upon the doctorate with little consideration of how picking up the stone would impact upon either my work or my professional identity. Thornton (2013) highlights that there are instances where social and personal senses of identity can come into conflict; where one's personal identity can jar with others' expectations; this is what happened in my case.

I viewed my teacher researcher identity as being, if not completely separate, then clearly distinct from my identity as a teacher, head of department and curriculum manager. I was being paid to do these jobs and I was not being paid to be a researcher; so, ethically, this separation was important (Glen, 2000). Yet Anderson and Herr (2010) suggest that practitioner knowledge is developed through a combination of tacit knowledge (acquired through years of practice) and formal knowledge (acquired through, amongst other things, professional reading). Essentially, the identities of teacher and researcher need to intersect and entwine in order for formal knowledge to develop alongside tacit knowledge. Engaging in research provided the opportunity to reflect and think critically about my practice; in short, I believe it allowed me to become a better geography teacher (Doncaster & Lester, 2002; Lester, 2004).

The continual struggle of balancing the different parts of my identity, to keep them separate but to enable them to co-exist, was made more challenging by the critical perspective of some colleagues. I could only see the positive individual benefits of my increased practitioner knowledge and the subsequent organisational benefits which occurred as a result (Lester, 2004). However, others commented that I had taken too much on, that the research and my part-time status were compromising my ability to be a leader and manager. My identity as a practitioner researcher, as well as creating internal tensions, encouraged external collisions between others' lives and environments (Atkinson-Baldwyn, 2009; Fenge, 2010). I felt frustrated that, despite a confidence in my own abilities to juggle the various aspects of my life, my identities of parent, manager, researcher and teacher seemed conflicting to others (Stryker & Burke, 2000; Colbeck, 2008).

This triggered a period of contemplation and reflection about my context and my future as a practitioner researcher. I had assumed that I would always teach and yet I was struggling to reconcile the different aspects of my identity both internally and externally. If my researcher identity was not valued within the context in which I had picked up the stone, did that matter? Cast (2003, p. 45) suggests that, "When individuals are confronted with a persistent mismatch between identity meanings and perceptions of the social environment, one possibility is simply to exit the role". In the event, this is what I chose to do. As a teacher, I struggled with my identity as a researcher because others did not see the value in it and I struggled with my identity as a parent because teaching was all-consuming. The resolution of this situation came with changing my job and leaving classroom teaching. I am now Secondary Curriculum Leader at the Geographical Association, a UK-based subject association which works with geography teachers in all phases of education. This new role provides an opportunity to design and lead continuing professional development programmes for geography teachers, to develop teacher networks and to write articles for the Association's publications for practitioners. My new position satisfies both the practitioner and researcher aspects of my identity and provides balance between them.

The change in my professional life has also given me a different perspective on my research. Whilst I still have to fit my research around my day job, there are more opportunities for overlap between the two, something which Barnet and Hyde (2001) and Colbeck (2008) identify as a catalyst for reducing stress and increasing mental well-being. In addition, whilst I collected the data for my research as a relative insider, I have now been given the opportunity to stand back and view from the perspective of a relative outsider (Griffiths, 1998; Kemmis, 2012). It has allowed me to stand in different positions around the pond, which has given me a more holistic understanding of its contours and a deeper appreciation of how the ripples of impact will travel.

What Ripples Does My Stone Have the Potential to Make? (or, What Are the Wider Impacts of Carrying Out Professional Doctoral Research Such as This?)

Engaging in a professional doctorate has had a huge, complicated and not always comfortable impact on my identity, both personally and professionally. It has resulted in my movement around the research pond and has enabled me to become more adept at looking critically at my practice. However, something that has always concerned me within the context of my research is the extent to which this research has the ability to make an impact on others and to result in change. In this section I therefore consider the wider impacts of the research on the students who were the focus of my study, the school in which the research was conceived and other members of the Geography Education Research community pond in which the stone will either generate ripples of impact or sink without trace.

What Are the Potential Wider Impacts on the Students?

As Gilbert (1994) and Rose (1997) explain in the context of creating geographical knowledge, the relationship between researcher and researched should be made visible and open to debate in order to be both reflexive and to highlight the dynamics of power inherent in the research. The eight students in my research all had varying experiences of geography as a school subject and of being taught by me. However, it remained ethically important to be clear and transparent to the students and to explain that their choice to be involved or not in the research would have no impact on their studies (Oliver, 2003; Alderson & Morrow, 2004). Yet how could I be so confident in this claim? They were giving up their time and, although I had outlined the scale of the task, I was concerned that they might find their participation burdensome. In the event it appeared that being involved in the research did have an impact on some students' studies but this was seen by them to be a positive thing. Two students who were taking A level Geography found the process of creating the collage useful to distil for themselves what they understood by geographical knowledge and to articulate the synoptic links that they observed; a skill critical for success at A level. They were surprised by some aspects that they had selected and the research gave them the opportunity to voice this. In addition, several students asked questions about what I was doing and why. They were genuinely interested in understanding why a busy professional would take on a research project. This became a leveller in the dynamics of power between myself and the students as this unprompted discussion created a common connection; we were all grappling with the challenge of academic demands.

What Are the Wider Impacts on My School?

The stimulus for this research was something very personal, it was happening in my classroom in my school and it is very important for me to share my findings in the context in which it was originally conceived and carried out. At a departmental level within this school, if this research can shed understanding on the aspects which influence student choices, features could be addressed which are within the teachers' control in an attempt to be more inclusive and increase uptake within those groups which are under-represented. For example, a strong theme in my data is negativity associated with geography fieldwork that is, any component of the curriculum that involves leaving the classroom and learning through first-hand experience (Boyle et al., 2007). This is unsurprising given that geography fieldwork, and physical geography fieldwork, in particular, is projected and experienced as a White and masculine 'heroic' endeavour (Driver, 1992; Rose, 1993; Kobayashi, 1994; Valentine, 1997). However, as Bracken and Mawdsley (2004) suggest, by designing fieldwork experiences, methods of data collection and analysis that are more likely to utilise skills and occur in spaces and places in which women are more comfortable, more positive accounts and perspectives of geography fieldwork can be 'reclaimed'.

Whilst I struggle a little with the term 'social justice' – being an activist scholar in the critical tradition does not sit comfortably with me, neither is the aim of the research to explicitly reveal and combat inequality and injustice – I do find the principles of Griffiths (1998) helpful in outlining the potential impacts of my research with the school context. The first principle she outlines is that there is no one right answer, no utopia, and that establishing social justice is less about particular outcomes and more about process. By picking up the stone I believe that I have started the process of reflection and the discussion about ethnic minority perspectives and choices. However, as a socially just state of affairs requires continual checking and adjusting it is no use for a solitary thrower to throw a single stone into the pond. What is needed is an environment where small-scale research is encouraged and celebrated and I would like the legacy of this research to be that other practitioners are given the confidence to have a go at throwing similar stones.

The second principle outlined is that each individual is valuable and recognised as an important part of the community as a whole. When discussing my research with others teachers it was interesting that the dominant view was that cultural and parental influence had the greatest significance for ethnic minority students when considering option choices and therefore what benefit did an enhanced awareness of this provide? In short, why research something that appears so obvious and that teachers can do nothing about? At best I think this view misses the point and, at worst is dangerous. It does not adhere to Griffith's second principle, assumes a simplistic and homogenous narrative for 25% of the school population and comes from a predominantly White, adult, male perspective. I am clear that my findings do not attempt to develop a typology of students of different ethnicities and their particular perspectives. However, what my findings have the potential to do is to challenge the dominant view and to value individual stories.

The third and final principle is that social justice is concerned not only with individual empowerment but also with structural injustices; that some individuals, communities or parts of communities have greater power and resources than others. Is it the stuctural decisions that the school, geography department and individual teachers make which serve to engender social injustice? In this regard my findings pose rather than answer questions around the selection of topics within the parameters of examination specifications and the structuring of option blocks from which students can select their subjects for study. However, simply asking these questions begins to challenge the status quo and to disrupt the accepted school structures within which students and teachers operate.

What Are the Wider Impacts for Geography Education Research?

Arguably, this research has the greatest potential to create widespread ripples if the new knowledge that it creates resonates with teachers in other contexts and with the gaps in knowledge identified by the Geography Education Research community. Having a role for an organisation with a prominent national and international reach has certainly made the first of these considerations more straightforward. My day job provides enormous potential for both the dissemination of my research findings and discussion with teachers to determine areas of resonance and dissonance with their own practice. In terms of identifying gaps in knowledge, over the last decade several researchers have attempted to outline these and to chart the contours of the pond into which the stone is headed.

Lambert (2015) identifies priorities drawn from a US context (Bednarz et al., 2013) which include learning progressions (including assessment), effective teaching, exemplary curricula and the impact of fieldwork. However, Roberts (2009) identifies learners' prior understandings of concepts in human geography, learners' use and understanding of resources other than maps, processes of teaching and learning in real-life classroom situations and the investigation of issues through a range of scales, for example, from national policy to how it impacts on learning in the classroom, as matters of neglect.

Whilst superficially this research on the perceptions of geographical knowledge and the stories students have relating to option choices may not appear to fit neatly within any of these identified priorities, its potential power lies in the fact that my findings weave through many of them. They get to the heart of discussions about the nature of subjects, students' perspectives and experiences and who makes the decisions about what is taught and how.

Last Ripples

Whilst acknowledging that all research journeys are unique there are recurring themes – both professional and personal – identified in the literature (Burgess & Wellington, 2010; Burgess et al., 2011). It is hoped that by starting a conversation with other practitioner researchers, by sharing my experiences and others engaging with the points of similarity or difference, the professional doctoral journey can be more consciously navigated. Certainly, the process of writing this chapter has been personally transformative. At the start, the open, exploratory research approach was problematic. I felt uncomfortable when considering whether my research would make metaphorical ripples or splashes as I was struggling to articulate to myself, let alone others, what the potential impacts of the findings could be. However, grappling with notions of identity and impact and discussion with others has enabled my appreciation of alternative discourses and a realisation that I was seeing 'impact' and 'change' in a singular, tangible and definite way. My research aims to shine a light on students' stories in order to move away from a single ethnic narrative, and writing this chapter has made me realise that it is shining a light where there was not one before (Martin, 2012).

Small-scale and context specific research, such as that described in this chapter, is more likely to generate small, localised ripples rather than sudden, transformative splashes of impact. Theoretically, the ripples move outwards with the greatest interest being shown by those working in the same organisation and a diminishing impact on those outside the organisation as the research findings move outwards. However, in reality, professional doctorates are rarely aligned with whole organisation priorities making it challenging for the researcher to maximise the impact of ripples closest to the stone. Re-focusing the emphasis of practitioner research on an 'organisational problem to be solved' encourages more staff to become stakeholders so that the ripples triggered are potentially broader and deeper.

Once instigated, the next challenge is to make the ripples travel as widely as possible. Again, this is not an easy task, partly because of the difficulties in generalising and extrapolating small-scale research to different contexts; the messages may or may not resonate. However, practitioner researchers can put themselves in a position to amplify the ripples and to ensure that the findings are disseminated widely. Davis et al. (2007) suggest that researchers' ability to do this is likely to depend upon whether they believe their findings are worthwhile, their level of confidence in the research, their interest in developing their profile within the fields of practice and research and whether the research was designed as a means of career advancement.

The reality of researching is however, rarely straightforward. Most researchers spend many years on their doctorates and the constituent parts do not stand still. Indeed, one of the most exciting parts of being a practitioner researcher is that you are working in the real world with all its messiness, complexity and dynamism. There is also the likelihood of 'real time impact' where the process of researching results in a clear and discernible change before the stone gets anywhere near the pond. Even if you do not change your context half way through the process, as I did, the essence of what you are investigating at the beginning is likely to be very different by the time you get to the end. By recognising, acknowledging and planning for this, the practitioner researcher is much better placed to control the strength and direction of the ripples and ensure that the stone does not sink without trace.

Concluding Comments

The writing of this chapter has come at a point in my research which could be perceived as problematic. Having analysed my data, I was poised to start writing up my findings and this had to be temporarily put on hold. It was also a challenge to work 'out of order'; to consider the impacts of my research before I had written about my findings. However, research is not a linear process, rather it is iterative, complex and messy. Rather than considering the impacts of my research at the end of my journey, I have been fortunate to have had the opportunity to think deeply about them in tandem with my analysis and I believe this has allowed me to think creatively in ways which I probably would not have otherwise done. In short, I feel that my final thesis will richer, more rounded and potentially have a greater impact as a result.

NOTES

[1] In the UK, as in many other countries, there are multiple doctoral routes (Neumann, 2005; Lester, 2004; Thomson and Walker, 2010). At the University of Cambridge, Faculty of Education where I am currently a graduate student there are two routes, the Doctorate of Philosophy (PhD) and the Doctorate of Education (EdD). Whilst they have many similarities, the EdD is a part-time professional doctorate which is "designed for experienced educational professionals, either practising teachers or those working in related fields (e.g. policy, advice and support or management), who are committed to extending their understanding through research and theorising policy or practice" (University of

Cambridge, Faculty of Education, 2016). For a comparison of the PhD and EdD doctoral routes at the University of Cambridge see http://www.educ.cam.ac.uk/courses/graduate/doctoral/

2   The school system in England is complex but broadly divided into Key Stages (KS) with Key Stages 1 and 2 forming Primary School and Key Stages 3–5 forming Secondary School. At my school, students in Key Stage 3 are aged 11–14 and study the National Curriculum where Geography is compulsory.

3   Students in Key Stage 4 are aged 15 to 16 and study for their General Certificate in Secondary Education (GCSE) in subjects that they have chosen to do. Students at my school typically choose to take between 10 and 13 subjects. English, Maths and Science are compulsory but students then choose their other subjects from a series of option blocks. Geography is in the Humanities option block along with History, Religious Studies and Business Studies and students have to select one or two of these subjects to study at GCSE level.

4   Students in Key Stage 5 are aged 17 to 18 and study for their AS and A levels again in subjects that they have chosen to do. Students at my school typically choose to take between 3 and 5 subjects from a pool of around 20. There are no subjects that are compulsory and whilst many students choose to take subjects that they have already studied at GCSE level, there are other subjects such as Politics and World Development which can be taken with no previous study.

REFERENCES

Adichie, C. (2009). *The danger of a single story.* Retrieved January 18, 2013, from http://www.ted.com/talks/chimamanda_adichie_the_danger_of_a_single_story.html

Alderson, P., & Morrow, V. (2004). *Ethics, social research and consulting with children and young people* (2nd ed.). Ilford: Barnardo's.

Anderson, G., & Herr, K. (2010). Generating practitioner knowledge through practitioner action research: Moving from local to public knowledge. In P. Thomson & M. Walker (Eds.), *The Routledge doctoral student's companion.* Abingdon: Routledge.

Atkinson-Baldwyn, L. (2009). An other identity: A view of myself. *Qualitative Inquiry, 15*(5), 806–819.

Bar-Gal, B., & Sofer, S. (2010). Israeli students' perceptions of geography instruction goals. *International Research in Geographical and Environmental Education, 19*(2), 127–137.

Barnett, R., & Hyde, J. (2001). Women, men, work, and family: An expansionist theory. *American Psychologist, 56*, 781–796.

Bednarz, S., Heffron, S., & Huynh, N. (Eds.). (2013). *A roadmap for 21st century geography education research. A report from the geography education research committee.* Washington, DC: Association of American Geographers. Retrieved January 21, 2016, from http://education.nationalgeographic.org/programs/road-map-project/

Biddulph, M. (2011). Articulating student voice and facilitating curriculum agency. *The Curriculum Journal, 22*(3), 381–399.

Boyle, A., Maguire, S., Martin, A., Milsom, C., Nash, R., Rawlinson, S., Turner, A., Wurthmann, S., & Conchie, S. (2007). Fieldwork is good: Student perception and the affective domain. *Journal of Geography in Higher Education, 31*(2), 299–317.

Bracken, L., & Mawdsley, E. (2004). 'Muddy glee': Rounding out the picture of women and physical geography fieldwork. *Area, 36*(3), 280–286.

Brown, A. (2010). *What's worth asking and why?, The Routledge doctoral student's companion.* Abingdon: Routledge.

Burgess, H., Weller, G., & Wellington, J. (2011). Tensions in the purpose and impact of professional doctorates. *Work-Based Learning E-Journal, 2*(1), 1–20.

Burgess, H., & Wellington. J. (2010). Exploring the impact of the professional doctorate on students' professional practice and personal development: Early indications. *Work Based Learning E-journal, 1*(1), 160–176.

Cast, A. (2003). Identities and behavior. In J. Burke, T. Owens, R. Serpe, & P. Thoits (Eds.), *Advances in identity theory and research.* New York, NY: Kluwer Academic/Plenum.

Catling, S. (2015). Getting underway with your research. In G. Butt (Ed.), *Master class in geography education: Transforming teaching and learning*. London: Bloomsbury.

Colbeck, C. (2008). Professional identity development theory and doctoral education. *New Directions for Teaching and Learning, 113*, 9–16.

College of Teachers. (2013). *The Teacher Learning Academy (TLA)*. Retrieved April 13, 2013, from http://www.collegeofteachers.ac.uk/tla

Davis, P., Hamilton, M., & James, K. (2007). *Maximising the impact of practitioner research: A handbook of practical advice*. London: Institute of Education.

Doncaster, K., & Lester, S. (2002). Capability and its development: Experiences from a work-based doctorate. *Studies in Higher Education, 27*(1), 91–101.

Driver, F. (1992). Geography's empire: Histories of geographical knowledge. *Environment and Planning D: Society and Space, 10*, 23–40.

Fenge, L. (2010). Sense and sensibility: Making sense of a professional doctorate. *Reflective Practice, 11*(5), 645–656.

Gilbert, M. (1994). The politics of location: Doing feminist research 'at home'. *Professional Geographer, 46*, 90–96.

Glen, S. (2000). The dark side of purity or the virtues of double-mindedness? In H. Simon & R. Usher (Eds.), *Situated ethics in educational research*. London: Routledge Falmer.

Green, B., & Lee, A. (1995). Theorising postgraduate pedagogy. *Australian Universities' Review, 38*(2), 40–45.

Griffiths, M. (1998). *Educational research for social justice: Getting off the fence*. Buckingham: Open University Press.

Herman, C. (2010). *Emotions and being a doctoral student. The Routledge doctoral student's companion*. Abingdon: Routledge.

John, M. (2003). *Children's rights and power: Charging up for a new century*. London: Jessica Kinsley Publishers.

Kemmis, S. (2012). Researching educational praxis: Spectator and participant perspectives. *British Educational Research Journal, 38*(6), 885–906.

Kenway, J., & McLeod, J. (2004). Bourdieu's reflexive sociology and 'spaces of points of view': Whose reflexivity, which perspective? *British Journal of Sociology of Education, 25*(4), 525–544.

Kitchen, R. (2013a). What is geography? The view from Year 7. *Teaching Geography, 38*(1), 17–19.

Kitchen, R. (2013b). Student perceptions of geographical knowledge and the role of the teacher. *Geography, 8*(3), 112–122.

Kobayashi, A. (1994). Coloring the field: Gender, 'race' and the politics of fieldwork. *Professional Geographer, 46*, 73–80.

Lambert, D. (2015). Research in geography education. In G. Butt (Ed.), *Masterclass in geography education: Transforming teaching and learning*. London: Bloomsbury.

Lave, J., & Wenger, E. (1991). *Situated learning. Legitimate peripheral participation*. London: Cambridge University Press.

Lester, S. (2004). Conceptualising the practitioner doctorate. *Studies in Higher Education, 29*(6), 757–770.

Martin, F. (2012). The geographies of difference. *Geography, 97*(3), 116–122.

Neumann, R. (2005). Doctoral differences: Professional doctorates and PhDs compared. *Journal of Higher Education Policy and Management, 27*(2), 173–188.

Oliver, P. (2003). *A students' guide to research ethics*. Maidenhead: Open University Press.

Petersen, E. (2007). Negotiating academicity: Postgraduate research supervision as category boundary work. *Studies in Higher Education, 32*(4), 475–487.

Roberts, M. (2009). *GTIP orientation piece – research*. Retrieved January 21, 2016, from http://www.geography.org.uk/gtip/orientationpieces/research/

Roberts, M. (2010). What is 'evidence-based practice' in geography education? *International Research in Geographical and Environmental Education, 19*(2), 91–95.

Rose, G. (1993). *Feminism and geography: The limits of geographical knowledge*. Cambridge: Polity Press.

Rose, G. (1997). Situating knowledges: Positionality, reflexivities and other tactics. *Progress in Human Geography, 21*(3), 305–320.

Scott, D., Brown, A., Lunt, I., & Thorne, L. (2004). *Professional doctorates: Integrating professional and academic knowledge*. Maidenhead: Open University Press.

Singleton, A. (2012). The geodemographics of access and participation in Geography. *The Geographical Journal, 178*(3), 216–229.

Stryker, S., & Burke, P. (2000). The past, present, and future of an identity theory. *Social Psychology Quarterly, 63*, 284–297.

Thomson, P., & Walker, M. (2010). Doctoral education in context: The changing nature of the doctorate and doctoral students. In P. Thomson & M. Walker (Eds.), *The Routledge doctoral student's companion*. Abingdon: Routledge.

Thornton, A. (2013). *Artist, researcher, reacher: A study of professional identity in art and education*. Bristol: Intellect.

University of Cambridge, Faculty of Education. (2016). *Doctoral paths*. Retrieved March 11, 2016, from http://www.educ.cam.ac.uk/courses/graduate/doctoral/

Valentine, G. (1997). Ode to a geography teacher 1: Sexuality and the classroom. *Journal of Geography in Higher Education, 21*, 417–424.

Van Maanen, J. (1988). *Confessional tales, tales of the field: On writing ethnography*. Chicago, IL: Chicago University Press.

Vidal Rodeiro, C. (2009). *Uptake of GCSE and A-level subjects in England by Ethnic Group 2007* (Statistics Report Series No. 11). Cambridge: Cambridge Assessment. Retrieved March 14, 2014, from http://www.cambridgeassessment.org.uk/Images/109903-uptake-of-gcse-and-a-level-subjects-in-england-by-ethnic-group-2007.pdf

Wagner, J. (2010) Ignorance in educational research: How not knowing shapes new knowledge. In P. Thomson & M. Walker (Eds.), *The Routledge doctoral student's companion*. Abingdon: Routledge.

Weeden, P. (2011). *An investigation into changing patterns of entry for GCSE geography: Choice, diversity and competition* (Unpublished PhD thesis). University of Birmingham, England.

Weick, K. (1995). *Sensemaking in organizations*. Thousand Oaks, CA: Sage.

Wellington, J. (2010). Weaving the threads of doctoral research journeys. In P. Thomson & M. Walker (Eds.), *The Routledge doctoral student's companion*. Abingdon: Routledge.

Wellington, J., & Sikes, P. (2006). A doctorate in a tight compartment: Why do students choose a professional doctorate and what impact does it have on their personal and professional lives? *Studies in Higher Education, 31*(6), 723–734.

RIIKKA HOFMANN

11. LEADING PROFESSIONAL CHANGE THROUGH RESEARCH(ING)

Conceptual Tools for Professional Practice and Research

INTRODUCTION

A woman and a small child are waiting for a lift in a department store. One of the lifts is out of order. The child looks at the broken lift, visibly stuck between two floors, and says: "*Mum, what do you think the lift is saying now?*"

Asking unusual and interesting questions and making original connections that make us (adults) notice new things about our world is typically considered a sign of intelligent thinking in children. As we become encultured into various expert practices and communities, it becomes increasingly difficult to ask such questions and escape our taken-for-granted assumptions and habits. When I ask professional graduate students to think of an example of something that made them gain a genuinely novel perspective on their practice, they often struggle. Research(ing) is about contributing novel insights through a process of systematic engagement with our world, led by the generation of focused, informed and worthwhile questions. Research in and on professional practice can make a significant contribution by enabling us to ask questions about habituated professional practice which can render previously taken-for-granted aspects of it available for critical reflection. Moreover, research is one central means to challenge our existing practices. This is no benign business. Deconstructing, and making choices between, practices, stepping into unknown worlds, is risky (cf. Hofmann, 2008a; Engeström, 1996). However, research on distributed leadership and collaborative school improvement shows that through focused sustained collaboration, it is possible to (re-)construct new 'envisioned ideologies' for the shared practice, and new professional identities within it (Rainio & Hofmann, 2015; see also MacBeath & Dempster, 2009).

This chapter explores the impact from research in and on professional practice on leadership, policy and scholarship. It is written with a view to those conducting professional doctorates, but addresses anyone attempting to effect and/or study professional change in education, medicine, nursing, social work or other fields. Current political debate demands that professionals in various fields become more engaged in (the outcomes and processes of) research. This chapter starts by taking a step back and considering why engaging in research(ing) is worthwhile for

P. Burnard et al. (Eds.), Transformative Doctoral Research Practices for Professionals, 141–154.
© 2016 Sense Publishers. All rights reserved.

practitioners second section. Discussing widely observed challenges in changing established professional practice, the third section sketches a role for close-up research in and on professional practice in individual settings in the current policy landscape, emphasising evidence-based practice. The fourth section will argue that researching (in) practice needs 'theory', drawing some possible theoretical lines to inform such research. Taking up challenges identified in the third section, the fifth section will illustrate actual conceptual tools through example studies. The chapter will conclude by arguing that, far from educational research being the 'problem child' of evidence-based policy and practice, it has a huge amount to offer to a range of professional fields. With its conceptual and methodological tools capable of scrutinising complex practices, and processes and mechanisms of professional change, in a way that grounds them in (what is feasible in) concrete institutional settings, educational research can make a real contribution to professional practice and leadership, policy and knowledge.

(WHY) DOES PROFESSIONAL PRACTICE REALLY NEED RESEARCH(ING)?

The principle of evidence-based practice has transformed medicine in the last two decades, and current policy in the U.K. and internationally emphasises the use of research (evidence) to inform professional practice in education, nursing and social work (Hantrais, Lenihan, & MacGregor, 2015; Haynes, Goldacre, Torgerson, & others, 2012). The debates around evidence-based policy are beyond the scope of this chapter (e.g., Wiseman, 2010). This chapter takes a two-fold perspective on this trend; firstly, as the policy context framing practitioners', professional leaders' (and researchers') current work (cf. Chapter 9, and, secondly, as a perspective which has brought to light how poorly we understand professional practice and change (e.g., Greenhalgh, Howick, & Maskrey, 2014; Shojania & Grimshaw, 2005). This chapter focuses on aspects of professional practices which cannot easily be prescribed by single guidelines. In education, Bassey (1992) talks about educational practitioners *creating* education. Even in professions with extensive evidence-based guidelines for decision-making, such as medicine, professionals now rarely simply 'deliver' treatments. Often, diagnosing and treating patients involves the negotiation and interpretation not only of multiple forms of clinical evidence, but of different value systems, interpersonal relationships and multiple fields of expertise and institutional structures (Greenhalgh et al., 2014; Shojania & Grimshaw, 2005). The same complexities apply to education, nursing and social work alike (Burton, Lepp, Morrison, & O'Toole, 2015; Edwards, 2011).

What contribution can researching those practices make, in addition to professionals' intuitive thinking and established professional knowledge and expertise (and prescriptive guidelines)? Especially, how can joint activity be concerted in a professional setting in which leadership enabling learning and engagement with evidence can emerge (cf. Gronn, 2002)? Research examining professional conversations in the workplace has found that sustaining a disciplined focus on learning and evidence in such conversations can be a challenge (Earl & Timperley, 2009; Rainio & Hofmann, 2015; Stein & Spillane, 2005; Swaffield & Dempster, 2009). This chapter argues that the nature of social practice and human intuition mean that professional practice – including how and why professional guidelines are (not) implemented – cannot be fully and systematically understood and explored without research.

Human reasoning is oriented towards recognising patterns. While pattern-recognition can be very helpful to professional practice, research has demonstrated how it also leads to systematic errors in intuitive reasoning. We tend to over-estimate the significance of patterns, for example where individual observations concur with prior assumptions or recent observations, form a one-off cluster or resemble a stereotype (Tversky & Kahneman, 1974; Gilovich & Griffin, 2002). This makes the systematic questioning of professional observations and reasoning valuable. Research can offer alternative 'heuristics' which can support thoughtful reinterpretation and reformulation of local practice (Ruthven, 2005).

There are also limitations to simply asking people for their perspective (cf. Rudduck, & Flutter, 2000) to sustain educative conversations (Hofmann, 2008a). For example, it has often been suggested that students wish for choice and autonomy in their learning. In my study exploring children's perspectives (Hofmann, 2008a), they indeed expressed a general preference for activities involving choice. However, when such talk was examined systematically in the context of the actual concrete activities the pupils had participated in, what made those activities meaningful to them was not simply about being able to choose. Rather, for example, a task that involved choice led to different students doing different topics, and hence gaining an authentic audience when presenting their work in class (Hofmann, 2008b). Such understandings influence the ways in which the practice could become more engaging and meaningful to students. This insight was made possible by the conceptual understanding of 'experience' as the meanings people give to activities (Engeström, 2003; Hofmann, 2008a), and the systematic comparison of multiple 'experiences' in the context of concrete examples of practice (Hofmann, 2008b).

Finally, socially and culturally established norms shape what we can do and 'see' in social practice and how we 'hear' what other people say. Discursive conventions are so integral to our thinking that they are not simply available for individuals to perceive as optional. For example, common conversational norms mean that even a short silence is poorly tolerated in conversation (Jefferson, 1988; cf. McHoul, 1978). Therefore, when asked a question, a colleague, student or patient is likely to feel compelled to provide a swift answer even if they are unsure. These norms cannot be simply locally altered by 'telling' people they do not apply, and even unintentionally violating them may influence the acceptability, or success, of new strategies among professionals or the stakeholders they work with (cf. Hofmann, 2008a; Hofmann & Mercer, 2015).

Intuitive reasoning, tradition and expert professional thinking will continue to be central for any successful professional practice to enable quick decisions and smooth everyday practice; however, researching professional practice can make a distinct contribution to conducting and leading professional practice.

EXPLORING THE GAP BETWEEN RESEARCH AND PRACTICE IN DIFFERENT PROFESSIONAL FIELDS

In education, the calls for practitioners and their institutions to use and conduct research are not new (Hargreaves, 1996; McIntyre, 2005; Ruthven, 2005; Apelgren, Burnard, & Cabaroglu, 2015). Equally enduring are the criticisms about the perceived failure of educational research to influence professional practice and there have been repeated calls for following the example of evidence-based practice in medicine (Hargreaves, 1996; Goldacre, 2013). These debates are even more widely encountered in social policy. This section will make some observations about the contribution researching (in) practice, close-up, can make beyond the local practice.

In many professional areas, such as nursing, medicine and social work, the gap between research and practice has commonly been explained through a deficit model, relating to the knowledge and attitudes of practitioners themselves (e.g., Shojania & Grimshaw, 2005). In education the perceived failure of research to inform practice has often been blamed on the quality of evidence available. Educational research has been criticised for not being driven by problems relevant to practice, not being cumulative, and not being written in a way accessible to practitioners (Goldacre, 2013; Hargreaves, 1996). In medicine, the approach of evidence-based practice has radically altered both professional decision-making and outcomes, particularly with regard to clearly diagnosable single illnesses in otherwise broadly healthy patients (Grimshaw & Russell, 1993). However, it is worth looking a bit more closely at the challenges of implementing evidence in professional practice.

Interventionist research in education suggests that influencing interactional aspects of professional practice is very difficult, even with good quality evidence and associated professional development (Osborne, Simon, Christodoulou, Howell-Richardson, & Richardson, 2013; Ruthven et al., 2016; Webb, Nemer, & Ing, 2006). Even in medicine, with the increasing volume of evidence and patients with complex multiple conditions, there is concern regarding the challenges of changing the more complex aspects of professional practice (Greenhalgh et al., 2014; Shojania & Grimshaw, 2005). The first set of observed challenges relates to a failure to implement available evidence systematically. Various possible explanations have been discussed, involving disagreement with guidelines (Lugtenberg, Schaick, Westert, & Burgers, 2009), perceived organisational constraints and patient factors (Ellen et al., 2014; Gagnon et al., 2014; Shojania & Grimshaw, 2005). The second set of challenges relates to complex cases and practices. It is one thing to influence a once-off decision by a single professional based on high quality evidence-based guidelines. It is an entirely different matter to influence the *process* of professional practice in contexts which may involve multiple professional fields and cultures, patients and relatives with complex simultaneous needs, beliefs and wishes.

This leads to a significant distinction for planning research agendas, complementing trials and other systematic evaluations. In medicine and nursing research, it is increasingly suggested the problem is not (only, or even primarily) lack of knowledge or trials about the relative importance of different factors as barriers or supporting factors to professional change. Rather, there is a fundamental gap in our knowledge and understanding of what those factors are *like* (e.g., what constitutes 'context' (McCormack et al., 2002) or 'organisational readiness for change' (Gagnon et al., 2014)), what the *processes* and *mechanisms* by which they change may be, and how they link with what is *locally feasible and acceptable* in given institutional cultures and circumstances (French et al., 2012; Shojania & Grimshaw, 2005).

There has been a call for more close-up research on process, informed by, and generating, theory to develop conceptual and methodological tools for understanding complex aspects of professional practice and their sociocultural, relational and institutional settings (e.g., Edwards, 2011; Apelgren et al., 2015; French et al., 2012). This call is accompanied by a gaze towards educational research to offer conceptual and methodological tools for studying, professional learning in medicine, nursing and social work (Burton et al., 2015; Edwards, 2011; Greenhalgh et al., 2014).

To conclude, it is suggested here that the relationship between professional practice and research is interdependent. Professional practice is not only a user of research outcomes, or a test-bed for well-developed ideas, but an important partner in the *process* of searching to better understand the *processes and mechanisms* by which change does (or does not) happen in concrete settings. This also applies to the relationship between evidence-based fields (such as medicine) and fields often depicted as insufficiently evidence-based (such as education). The mutual learning opportunities between such fields are not always recognised in education policy discourse.

A ROLE FOR THEORY

In addition to understanding barriers to professional change, we need to understand how those barriers interact with the local professional setting and culture, as well as the potential pathways to, and mechanism of, change. Close-up research on and in professional practice has the opportunity to research these processes in their real settings, with an understanding of the local culture. Research in various professional fields suggests that even extensive opportunities to reflect on one's professional practice do not automatically, or even commonly, lead to changes in practice (Bakkenes, Vermunt, & Wubbels, 2010; Driessen, Van Tartwijk, Overeem, Vermunt, & Van Der Vleuten, 2005). Using theory can help practitioners ask novel questions about and gain new perspectives into their practice. Moreover, using and developing conceptual tools to characterise systematic observations of practice means that researchers of practice can go beyond informing and describing a single local practice, generating ideas and principles regarding that practice that can help other professionals and researchers to probe their practices and understandings.

The concepts and studies illustrated in the next section draw on theoretical approaches to social practice which recognise the role of language and sociocultural practice in learning. These involve cultural-historical activity theory, otherwise known under the acronym CHAT (Edwards, 2010; Engeström, 1999). This strand of theorising considers the historically accumulated *local practice in a particular professional and institutional setting* as integral to participants' actions in that setting. It emphasises the need to attend the *practitioners' collective and individual goals and motives* (ibid.). Focused on change, CHAT aims to be "an engaged social science which can make a difference" (Edwards, 2001, p. 162), making it a useful framework for researching and leading professional change. CHAT emphasises that what *matters* to practitioners centrally orients their interpretations and responses to practice (Edwards, 2010). It suggests that we need to pay attention to what the participants in a particular professional practice are trying to *do* through their interactions and what they are trying to get done (Hofmann, 2008a; Hofmann & Mercer, 2015), both collectively and individually.

The frameworks for the studies in the next section also involve theories focusing on the role of *language and discourse* in social practice (Blumer, 1969; Mercer, 2007; Sacks, 1995). As discussed above, research on social interaction has demonstrated how interactive settings have well established norms and rules. These norms can make the take up of new actions and strategies difficult. For example, while research in psychology and education has suggested that immediately evaluating students' responses in teaching settings does not support their thinking (e.g., Webb et al., 2006), interaction research has illustrated how students *expect* that evaluative feedback is offered on their contributions (cf. Sinclair & Coulthard, 1975). Hence professionals trying to change their *individual* practice alone may find this difficult in the context of normative expectations of colleagues, students, clients or patients.

We have argued that to present different ways of conducting professional practice, even when evidence-based, as alternatives which professionals could simply choose to use on any occasion would be naive and ignore the practical reasons *why* professionals, and institutions develop and maintain the practices that they do (Hofmann & Mercer, 2015). We need to examine the kinds of difficulties professionals may have in abandoning habituated strategies or ways of thinking in particular sociocultural and institutional settings (ibid.). Engaging with such theoretical approaches can help practitioners and those researching practice understand why such forms of interaction can be difficult to change even with evidence and a desire for change. In the next section I will discuss several examples of research on professional practice. While not practitioner-research, these studies serve to illustrate the various points made in this chapter.

CONCEPTUAL TOOLS FOR RESEARCHING (IN) PRACTICE AND PROFESSIONAL CHANGE

Three broad issues were identified in an earlier section as potential challenges for researchers, policy-makers and leaders trying to impact and understand professional change: (i) non-implementation of new ideas or strategies by practitioners; (ii) local institutional constraints; and (iii) unexpected outcomes of implementation. This section will discuss examples of conceptual tools that may illuminate aspects of those challenges. If 'decompositions' of professional practice – in professional education – make visible the 'grammar of practice' (Grossman et al., 2009), this section explores tools which seek to make visible the 'semantics' – meanings of practice – and 'pragmatics' – how context contributes to meaning. Main examples of practice are drawn from educational and medical settings; examples are related to a range of professional practices.

Attending to Practitioners' Local Goals

The first example concerns the discussion of factors relating to why practitioners may not implement new research-based ideas. I will illustrate one aspect of this puzzle through a close-up study of secondary mathematics and science teachers taking part in an intervention study which aimed to support the development of dialogic teaching methods (see Ruthven et al., 2016). Our study (Hofmann & Mercer, 2015) was interested in the ways in which teachers intervene during group work to support students' discussion and thinking. It was also interested in understanding how new research-informed strategies could become engaging for the professionals.

Our approach was informed by the theoretical understanding that proposals for changing professional practice need to be embedded in an understanding of what *motivates* that practice (Hofmann & Mercer, 2015; cf. Edwards, 2010). We combined this with the insight from research on professional practice suggesting that practitioners' knowledge and actions are oriented towards concrete and specific *problems of practice* (Ruthven, 2005). We focused on both the teachers' actions in, and their views of, their practice during group work in order to understand when and why teachers intervene in groups; and what these professionals themselves viewed as the concrete 'problems of this practice' that they were trying to work on. The perception of the 'problem' to be addressed by action in those situations may influence the kinds of intervention strategies that are perceived as appropriate and beneficial.

The study illustrated that the professionals' and researchers' reasons warranting an intervention in a group were not the same. For example, research suggests that correct responses (e.g., in mathematics) do not necessarily represent genuine understanding and require probing; however, we know that in actual (mathematics) classroom practice correct responses tend to be accepted at face value (e.g., Webb et al., 2006).

Our study noted that when a group had finished quickly and were proposing a correct solution, the primary problem perceived by many teachers was the need to keep the group *occupied* while other groups were still working, not to scrutinise the group's response. For new research-based strategies to be perceived as appropriate, they may need to align with the goals professionals hold *themselves* accountable for regarding a specific aspect of practice: for example, strategies of teacher intervention which would help to occupy a group effectively, yet meaningfully (in terms of developing students' understanding) (Hofmann & Mercer, 2015).

Such problems of practice refer to concrete and specific aspects of professional practice – not to general discourses (such as 'helping children learn' or 'making the patient better'). Beside reflection on local practice, this highlights an opportunity for wider impact from research in professional practice. Researching such local goals and perceived problems of practice within professionals' own institutions can support leadership for change. Furthermore, close-up insider professional research across such settings can contribute to our understanding of the range of local goals and successful pathways to aligning research and development goals with those of the practitioners. In the area of medicine or social work this may also involve not only seeking an understanding of what problems matter most to patients or clients, but ensuring responsive subsequent care. In increasingly multi-professional work, the sub-specialisation of professionals (e.g., Plochg, Klazinga, & Starfield, 2009) and limited understandings of how professionals outside one's own area think (cf. Edwards, 2011), mean that this perspective can go missing if not purposefully sought.

How Institutional 'Lived Ideologies' Shape Perceived Opportunities for Professional Change

Much research has focused on identifying barriers to professional change. However, there are limitations to enabling professional change through 'removing barriers' to change. Practitioners are readily able to offer reasons for not implementing new ideas (e.g., Hennessy, Hassler, & Hofmann, 2015). However, institutionally shared talk of barriers in a particular setting is not only about 'perceptions', but a way of making sense of, and dealing with, the complex situations in which participants find themselves (cf. Checkland, Harrison, & Marshall, 2007; Engeström, 2007). Shared and enduring ways of describing the local practice in a particular institutional setting have been conceptualised through the notion of 'lived ideologies': a 'common sense' that groups of people share in the local setting such as a workplace (Billig et al., 1988). This is not suggesting that professionals in a particular setting necessarily share a permanent set of beliefs, but rather that they recognise and use the same ways of conceptualising their professional practice and the contradictions it involves (Rainio & Hofmann, 2015).

Such established ways of talking about one's local practice are not only 'excuses' to avoid change. They shape understandings of what is possible and can influence what people can 'see'. For example, my research illustrated how, even when a teacher made systematic efforts to interrupt the cultural model of the teacher as having all the answers, through repeated attempts to convey to pupils the limits of their knowledge, children continued to draw on the dominant conceptualisation of the teacher as knower and failed to 'see' the teacher's efforts (Hofmann, 2008a). Without making those local 'ideologies' visible to participants, it is difficult to change the practice that they conceptualise.

In our study of staff conversations in a socially disadvantaged urban secondary school engaging in a school-led development programme, the characteristics of the students were constructed as something that had to be accepted and even 'respected' (their personalities, attitudes, local culture). Given the challenges around those characteristics, they hereby also became constructed as an obstacle for change. The object of the teachers' work in the school became one of 'coping' with the difficult (but 'inevitable') status quo; the shared narratives about their 'difficult students' helped them cope in those challenging circumstances. Gradually, in the process of systematically addressing and experimenting with these obstacles, the practitioners began to 'notice' opportunities for doing things differently. This, however, required a shift in their *collective* sense about the object of their (school's) work: From trying to cope with the difficult characteristics of their pupils which (indeed) inhibited teaching and learning, to collectively perceiving those characteristics as the target and content of their work (Rainio & Hofmann, 2015). Hence aiming to address named barriers to change without collectively understanding, and engaging with, the institutional common sense of which they are a part may not be successful (cf. Checkland et al., 2007). In nursing, for example, these ideas might relate to the local 'common sense' of their professional role as 'advocates' or 'experts' in a particular setting which might lead to differences in what new strategies and practices are perceived as possible and desirable.

Unintended Outcomes at the Intersections of Different Norms and Operating Principles Underlying Practice

However, research has shown that even when professionals implement new practices, the outcomes can be unexpected. Silverman's (1983) analysis of medical encounters at paediatric cleft palate clinics illustrated how, in conversations between the doctors and their teenage patients, the various norms and 'operating principles' (cf. Maine & Hofmann, 2016) at play meant that it was difficult for either participant to establish what they wanted. The doctors' talk drew on professional operating principles suggesting: (i) they should be friendly to the patient, (ii) cosmetic surgery should be the decision of the child, and (iii) decision for surgery should not be taken lightly. The teenage patients, on the other hand, were influenced by conversational and cultural norms suggesting that (i) greetings should be answered positively, not honestly ('hello how are you?'), that (ii) it is inappropriate to express preoccupation with one's looks and that (iii) medical talk is for doctors. In answering greetings positively

('I'm fine'), being non-committal about their looks and avoiding engagement in medical talk made it difficult for these patients, within the professional operating principles at place, to make it clear that they wanted cosmetic surgery (Silverman, 1983). Moreover, the intersection of the principles led to some situations in which children who did express overt concern about their looks were considered, by the professionals, as very confident and hence not actually needing surgery (Silverman, 1987 cited in Silverman, 2007).

There is nothing essentially wrong about the norms and operating principles at play here. It is the interaction between them, when not understood and made explicit, that can lead to problematic results. While many professionals working with people have become increasingly expert in the nuances of conversations with students, patients and clients, these kinds of in-built processes of misunderstanding are difficult to detect without theoretically informed close-up analysis in and on practice. Our research of teaching reading comprehension through small-group discussion tasks also illustrated this. Comparative close-up analysis of multiple incidences of the 'same' practice (the same reading comprehension task using the same research-informed model for supporting student discussions) showed how different underlying operating principles regarding the purposes of reading comprehension led to the new discussion strategies being appropriated for very different purposes (Maine & Hofmann, 2016).

Hence strategies used by professionals may be superficially recognisable as the same to practitioners themselves as well as developers, and hence often assumed to be doing the same 'thing' (e.g., Silverman's doctors genuinely queried the children's perspectives). It is only through close-up analytic engagement with local interactions that such important differences can be detected.

CLOSING REFLECTIONS

The starting point for the discussion in this chapter was the known dilemma that while research shows that learning-centred distributed leadership can make a difference to the professional practice in an organisation, it also shows that leading focused learning-centred professional conversations is difficult. We have explored how researching (in) professional practice and change can make a difference in and for organisations, and finally we turn to consider the implications of this interrelationship.

It has been argued in this chapter that professional practice can benefit not only from outcomes of research (including large-scale evaluations and intervention studies), but also from the process of researching practice and engaging with theory in relation to that practice. One of the ways in which research does so is by prompting professionals to challenge the taken-for-granted assumptions and habitual ways of thinking in their practice that may not otherwise be addressed. At the same time, this chapter has argued that the inter-relationship between research and practice is bi-directional and, in some sense, co-dependent. Research needs authentic examples of practice in order to understand – rather than assume – what the actual problems of practice are, how ideas are implemented in practice, particularly in complex 'cases', and how context influences meaning.

Policy has often held evidence-based fields (such as medicine) as an example for 'relational' fields (such as education). This chapter has argued that educational research on and in relational practices has much to contribute to evidence-based professions, such as medicine, especially in terms of conceptual and methodological tools for understanding human interaction and learning in complex circumstances.

These key points illustrate the many ways in which leading professional practice through research(ing) can be transformative (cf. Chapter 12). Theoretically-informed engagement with practice and with colleagues can enable genuinely novel perspectives on one's own and others' work that can contribute to making the implementation and development of new ideas possible (cf. Chapter 9). Moreover, the insights and conceptual tools that can be developed by systematic theoretically-informed engagement with local practice can make a real contribution to knowledge, both to other professionals and to scholarly knowledge. Such a contribution involves understanding the range of things that matter to, and norms that influence, practitioners in concrete activities in real institutional settings, and the ways in which these influence pathways to change. Such wider impact from local close-up research requires that the same conceptual tools – these or others – are systematically employed across multiple local settings to offer access to the range of issues involved in professional practice and the concrete ways in which such practice can change. I propose seeking to conduct more 'purposefully educative research' of professional practice: inquiry whose purpose is to relate not solely to improvement of local practice but to scholarship – but where opportunities to learn for those (actual people) participating in the study are an integral part (rather than a by-product, as often with purely academic research) of this process.

REFERENCES

Apelgren, B.-M., Burnard, P., & Cabaroglu, N. (2015). Theory-use in teacher research. In P. Burnard, B.-M. Apelgren, & N. Cabaroglu (Eds.), *Transformative teacher research: Theory and practice for the C21st* (pp. 3–12). Rotterdam, The Netherlands: Sense Publishers.

Bakkenes, I., Vermunt, J. D., & Wubbels, T. (2010). Teacher learning in the context of educational innovation: Learning activities and learning outcomes of experienced teachers. *Learning and Instruction, 20*(6), 533–548. Retrieved from http://doi.org/10.1016/j.learninstruc.2009.09.001

Bassey, M. (1992). Creating education through research. *British Educational Research Journal, 18*(1), 3–16.

Billig, M., Condor, S., Edwards, D., Gane, M., Middleton, D., & Radley, A. (1988). *Ideological dilemmas: A social psychology of everyday thinking.* London: Sage.

Blumer, H. (1969). *Symbolic interactionism: Perspective and method.* Englewood Cliffs, NJ: Prentice-Hall.

Burton, B., Lepp, M., Morrison, M., & O'Toole, J. (2015). Drama for learning in professional development contexts: A global perspective. In *Acting to manage conflict and bullying through evidence-based strategies* (pp. 119–141). Cham: Springer International Publishing. Dordrecht, The Netherlands: Springer.

Checkland, K., Harrison, S., & Marshall, M. (2007). Is the metaphor of "barriers to change" useful in understanding implementation? Evidence from general medical practice. *Journal of Health Services Research & Policy, 12*(2), 95–100. Retrieved from http://doi.org/10.1258/135581907780279657

Driessen, E. W., Van Tartwijk, J., Overeem, K., Vermunt, J. D., & Van Der Vleuten, C. P. M. (2005). Conditions for successful reflective use of portfolios in undergraduate medical education. *Medical Education, 39*(12), 1230–1235. Retrieved from http://doi.org/10.1111/j.1365-2929.2005.02337.x

Earl, L. M., & Timperley, H. (Eds.). (2009). *Professional learning conversations: Challenges in using evidence for improvement.* New York, NY: Springer.

Edwards, A. (2001). Researching pedagogy: A sociocultural agenda. *Pedagogy, Culture and Society, 9*(2), 161–186.

Edwards, A. (2010). *Being an expert professional practitioner: The relational turn in expertise* (Vol. 3). New York, NY: Springer.

Edwards, A. (2011). Building common knowledge at the boundaries between professional practices: Relational agency and relational expertise in systems of distributed expertise. *International Journal of Educational Research, 50*(1), 33–39.

Ellen, M. E., Léon, G., Bouchard, G., Ouimet, M., Grimshaw, J. M., & Lavis, J. N. (2014). Barriers, facilitators and views about next steps to implementing supports for evidence-informed decision-making in health systems: A qualitative study. *Implementation Science, 9*(1), 179.

Engeström, R. (2003). Sairauden kokemisen moniäänisyys terveydenhuollossa (Finn., The multivoicedness of experiencing illness in health care). In M.-L. Honkasalo, I. Kangas, & U. Seppälä (Eds.), *Sairas, potilas, omainen–Näkökulmia sairauden kokemiseen* (pp. 308–331). Helsinki: SKS.

Engeström, Y. (1996). Development as breaking away and opening up: A challenge to Vygotsky and Piaget. *Swiss Journal of Psychology, 55*(2–3), 126–132.

Engeström, Y. (1999). Activity theory and individual and social transformation. In Y. Engeström, R. Miettinen, & R.-L. Punamäki (Eds.), *Perspectives on activity theory* (pp. 19–38). Cambridge: Cambridge University Press.

Engeström, Y. (2007). From stabilization knowledge to possibility knowledge in organizational learning. *Management Learning, 38*(3), 271–275.

French, S. D., Green, S. E., O'Connor, D. A., McKenzie, J. E., Francis, J. J., Michie, S., Buchbinder, R., Schattner, P., Spike, N., & Grimshaw, J. M. (2012). Developing theory-informed behaviour change interventions to implement evidence into practice: A systematic approach using the Theoretical Domains Framework. *Implementation Science, 7*(1), 38. Retrieved from http://doi.org/10.1186/1748-5908-7-38

Gagnon, M.-P., Attieh, R., Ghandour, E. K., Légaré, F., Ouimet, M., Estabrooks, C. A., & Grimshaw, J. (2014). A systematic review of instruments to assess organizational readiness for knowledge translation in health care. *PloS One, 9*(12), e114338.

Gilovich, T., & Griffin, D. (2002). Introduction-heuristics and biases: Then and now. *Heuristics and Biases: The Psychology of Intuitive Judgment*, 1–18.

Goldacre, B. (2013). *Building evidence into education.* London: Department for Education.

Greenhalgh, T., Howick, J., & Maskrey, N. (2014). Evidence based medicine: A movement in crisis? *BMJ, 348*, g3725. Retrieved from http://doi.org/10.1136/bmj.g3725

Grimshaw, J. M., & Russell, I. T. (1993). Effect of clinical guidelines on medical practice: A systematic review of rigorous evaluations. *The Lancet, 342*(8883), 1317–1322. Retrieved from http://doi.org/10.1016/0140-6736(93)92244-N

Gronn, P. (2002). Distributed leadership as a unit of analysis. *The Leadership Quarterly, 13*(4), 423–451.

Grossman, P., Compton, C., Igra, D., Ronfeldt, M., Shahan, E., & Williamson, P. (2009). Teaching practice: A cross-professional perspective. *The Teachers College Record, 111*(9), 2055–2100.

Hantrais, L., Lenihan, A. T., & MacGregor, S. (2015). Evidence-based policy: Exploring international and interdisciplinary insights. *Contemporary Social Science, 10*(2), 101–113. Retrieved from http://doi.org/10.1080/21582041.2015.1061687

Hargreaves, D. (1996). *Teaching as a research-based profession: Possibilities and prospects (The Teacher Training Agency Lecture 1996).* London: Teacher Training Agency.

Haynes, L., Service, O., Goldacre, B., & Torgerson, D. (2012). Test, learn, adapt: Developing public policy with randomised controlled trials. *Cabinet Office-Behavioural Insights Team.* Retrieved from http://papers.ssrn.com/sol3/papers.cfm?abstract_id=2131581

Hennessy, S., Hassler, B., & Hofmann, R. (2015). Challenges and opportunities for teacher professional development in interactive use of technology in African schools. *Technology, Pedagogy and Education, 24*(5), 1–28.

Hofmann, R. (2008a). *Ownership in learning: A sociocultural perspective on pupil engagement, collaboration and agency in the classroom* (unpublished PhD dissertation). University of Cambridge, Cambridge.

Hofmann, R. (2008b). Rethinking "ownership of learning": Participation and agency in the storyline classroom. In S. Bell, S. Harkness, & G. White (Eds.), *Storyline: Past, present and future* (pp. 64–78). Glasgow: University of Strathclyde.

Hofmann, R. (in press). Book review of Finnish innovations and technologies in schools: A guide towards new ecosystems of learning by Niemi et al. *Teacher Development.*

Hofmann, R., & Mercer, N. (2015). Teacher interventions in small group work in secondary mathematics and science lessons. *Language and Education, 20*(3), 1–17. Retrieved from http://www.tandfonline.com/doi/abs/10.1080/13664530.2015.1131474#.V0qf1Hi9Kc0

Jefferson, G. (1988). Preliminary notes on a possible metric which provides for a 'standard maximum' silence of approximately one second in conversation. In D. Roger & P. Bull (Eds.), *Conversation: An interdisciplinary perspective.* Clevedon, UK: Multilingual Matters.

Lugtenberg, M., Schaick, J. M. Z., Westert, G. P., & Burgers, J. S. (2009). Why don't physicians adhere to guideline recommendations in practice? An analysis of barriers among Dutch general practitioners. *Implementation Science, 4*(1), 54. Retrieved from http://doi.org/10.1186/1748-5908-4-54

MacBeath, J. E. C., & Dempster, N. (2009). *Connecting leadership and learning: Principles for practice.* London: Routledge.

Maine, F., & Hofmann, R. (2016). Talking for meaning: The dialogic engagement of teachers and children in a small group reading context. *International Journal of Educational Research, 75*, 45–56.

McCormack, B., Kitson, A., Harvey, G., Rycroft-Malone, J., Titchen, A., & Seers, K. (2002). Getting evidence into practice: The meaning of "context." *Journal of Advanced Nursing, 38*(1), 94–104.

McHoul, A. (1978). The organization of turns at formal talk in the classroom. *Language in Society, 7*(2), 183–213.

McIntyre, D. (2005). Bridging the gap between research and practice. *Cambridge Journal of Education, 35*(3), 357–382. Retrieved from http://doi.org/10.1080/03057640500319065

Mercer, N. (2007). Sociocultural discourse analysis: Analysing classroom talk as a social mode of thinking. *Journal of Applied Linguistics and Professional Practice, 1*(2), 137–168.

Niemi, H., Multisilta, J., Lipponen, L., & Vivitsou, M. (2014). *Finnish innovations and technologies in schools: A guide towards new ecosystems of learning.* Rotterdam, The Netherlands: Sense Publishers.

Osborne, J., Simon, S., Christodoulou, A., Howell-Richardson, C., & Richardson, K. (2013). Learning to argue: A study of four schools and their attempt to develop the use of argumentation as a common instructional practice and its impact on students. *Journal of Research in Science Teaching, 50*(3), 315–347.

Plochg, T., Klazinga, N. S., & Starfield, B. (2009). Transforming medical professionalism to fit changing health needs. *BMC Medicine, 7*, 64. Retrieved from http://doi.org/10.1186/1741-7015-7-64

Rainio, A. P., & Hofmann, R. (2015). Transformations in teachers' discourse about their students during a school-led pedagogic intervention. *The European Journal of Social and Behavioural Sciences, 13*(2), 1815–1829.

Rudduck, J., & Flutter, J. (2000). Pupil participation and pupil perspective: 'carving a new order of experience'. *Cambridge Journal of Education, 30*(1), 75–89.

Ruthven, K. (2005). Improving the development and warranting of good practice in teaching. *Cambridge Journal of Education, 35*(3), 407–426.

Ruthven, K., Mercer, N., Taber, K., Guardia, P., Hofmann, R., Ilie, S., Luthan, S., & Riga, F. (2016). A research-informed dialogic-teaching approach to early secondary-school mathematics and science: The pedagogical design and field trial of the epiSTEMe intervention. *Research Papers in Education*, 1–23.

Sacks, H. (1995). *Lectures on conversation* (G. Jefferson & E. A. Schegloff, Ed.). Oxford: Blackwell.

Shojania, K. G., & Grimshaw, J. M. (2005). Evidence-based quality improvement: The state of the science. *Health Affairs, 24*(1), 138–150. Retrieved from http://doi.org/10.1377/hlthaff.24.1.138

Silverman, D. (1983). The clinical subject: Adolescents in a cleft-palate clinic. *Sociology of Health & Illness, 5*(3), 253–274.

Silverman, D. (2007). *A very short, fairly interesting and reasonably cheap book about qualitative research*. London: Taylor & Francis.

Sinclair, J. M., & Coulthard, M. (1975). *Towards an analysis of discourse: The English used by teachers and pupils*. London: Oxford University Press.

Stein, M. K., & Spillane, J. (2005). What can researchers on educational leadership learn from research on teaching? Building a bridge. In W. A. Firestone & C. Riehl (Eds.), *A new agenda for research in educational leadership* (pp. 28–45). New York, NY: Teachers College Press.

Swaffield, S., & Dempster, N. (2009). A learning dialogue. In *Connecting leadership and learning: Principles for practice*. London: Routledge.

Tversky, A., & Kahneman, D. (1974). Judgment under uncertainty: Heuristics and biases. *Science, 185*(4157), 1124–1131. Retrieved from http://doi.org/10.1126/science.185.4157.1124

Webb, N. M., Nemer, K. M., & Ing, M. (2006). Small-group reflections: Parallels between teacher discourse and student behavior in peer-directed groups. *The Journal of the Learning Sciences, 15*(1), 63–119.

Wiseman, A. W. (2010). The uses of evidence for educational policymaking: Global contexts and international trends. *Review of Research in Education, 34*(1), 1–24. Retrieved from http://doi.org/10.3102/0091732X09350472

CONCLUSION

JULIA FLUTTER

12. CONNECTING THE VOICES, JOURNEYINGS AND PRACTICES OF THE DOCTORATE FOR PROFESSIONALS

REFLECTING BACK

Having ventured through this book meeting with the voices, journeyings and practices that comprise our voyagers' various tales, we now arrive full circle and pick up the threads of themes which have emerged over the course of our travels. In this final chapter we draw these threads together to reflect on alternative ways of thinking about professional doctoral practices and to examine why these approaches to knowledge creation might be considered transformative, both within and beyond the students' own professional context. We start with looking at the question of purposes: what light do our narratives shed on the purposes of researching professional practice through a professional doctorate in education?

PURPOSES

At the beginning of this book we left a marker buoy to remind us that we would be returning to consider important questions surrounding the purposes of professional doctorate research later on. Each student author has offered differing, individual reasons why they chose to take up professional doctorate research but there are nonetheless commonalities across these accounts. A key purpose resonating through many of the narratives is to address specific problems within the student's professional context or to improve aspects of their own professional practice in diverse educational settings reflecting what Habermas (1971) refers to as a *practical* cognitive interest in research where the 'craft' of teaching and learning, whatever setting or context these occur within, is examined. However, some contributors' work exemplifies the *technical* cognitive interest, a term Habermas used to describe research that seeks to develop knowledge at the theoretical level, generating causal understandings. The professional doctorate affords opportunities for applying research tools that allow the general and local to be explored and understood via a process similar to reversing the telescope, looking back and forth at the micro level (local) and the macro level (general). The positioning of a professional doctorate researcher at the nexus of practice and theory places them at a unique vantage point, as Riikka Hofmann argues in Chapter 11.

P. Burnard et al. (Eds.), Transformative Doctoral Research Practices for Professionals, 157–161.

For others the purpose of their research may align more closely with Habermas' notion of *transformative* or *emancipatory* cognitive interest in research which calls for approaches centered on interpretation and critique. Karen Ottewell, for example in Chapter 3, describes her reasons for undertaking a second doctorate like this: "... my primary motivation to do a professional doctorate is simply that this will provide me with a framework of critical reflexivity through which I will be able to research my own and my community's professional practice with a view to being better at my job". Chapter 3's co-author, Wai Mun Lim defines the purpose of her own research as being to, "...develop a framework of value that could be co-created between the various stakeholders..." linking her aims and approach with a collaborative purpose that moves beyond immediate problem-solving. For James Knowles in Chapter 7 the question of purpose is also connected with issues of personal fulfilment: "To me professional doctorate research is about changing thinking, about how we do things, thinking about who we are, who we want to become, how we can do things better and even how we can live more fulfilled lives".

WATER

As the cover image to this book reminds us, our voyages are water-borne and the metaphor of water connects two key dimensions of the voices, journeyings and practices of the doctorate for professionals. One dimension is the flow of ideas that are encountered within the professional doctorate experience. At a personal level, this creative flow is experienced as exhilarating and life-enhancing according to psychologist, Mihaly Csikszentmihalyi:

> The best moments in our lives are not the passive, receptive, relaxing times...
> The best moments usually occur if a person's body or mind is stretched to its limits in a voluntary effort to accomplish something difficult and worthwhile.
> (1990, p. 3)

Water, inert and almost invisible until it moves, attains a force that can re-shape mountains once set in motion. Of course, not all our contributors sought ground-breaking impact for their research but, as we saw in Chapter 9, impact can be difficult to predict or control. The ripples emanating from the tiny droplet in our cover image remind us of the circles of influence emergent from our students' work, expanding outwards towards as yet unknown destinations.

The other dimension of our water metaphor lies in its expression of the fluidity in identity which our contributors speak of in describing their experiences of becoming professional doctorate students. Opening one's self to new ways of thinking and ways of being is profoundly challenging and unsettling, as our contributors' stories show, but it is only through letting go and trusting the waters of learning that these journeys have achieved their ends.

TRAVELLING

The concept of travelling, of starting at one point and moving to the next, is fundamental to all learning processes and it is important to remember that research is integral to that forward movement, propelling us towards new knowledge, new capacities and new ways of seeing ourselves. Fittingly, some chapters even refer to the physical journeys which students made during the course of their studies and, in James Knowles' case, even to living temporarily in a vehicle. James's vivid, personal account describes how researching his professional practice lead not only to profound changes in his personal and professional identities, but also extended to changing his students' lives and learning: "An important consideration for researching professionals in education, ...is that we can influence our students through what we have learnt during professional doctorate research" (Chapter 7).

But our contributors' stories also reveal the tensions and challenges, and sometimes upheavals, which occurred during the course of their research. In particular, the uncomfortable sense of exposure – of being outside one's habitus – is a strikingly recurrent theme. We heard, for example, how Simon Dowling (Chapter 4) and Gavin Turner (Chapter 6) grappled with ethical and methodological dilemmas inherent to positioning themselves as researching practitioners. Such journeys may prove to be worthwhile but, as Riikka Hofmann observes in Chapter 11, this stepping into "unknown worlds is risky". Some of our researching professionals' stories suggest how encountering new ideas, and embracing a willingness to accept one's identity as being 'fluid', through engagement in a professional doctorate programme can prove to be transformative and emancipatory. Moreover, becoming part of a community of researching professionals representing a diversity of disciplines creates a space in which such risk-taking can be encouraged, leading towards "...cognitive flexibility, manifested in a willingness to see beyond one's own discipline and to the integration of knowledge" (Segalas Coral & Tejedor Papell, 2016, p. 205).

DESTINATIONS

Our final theme is concerned with the destinations at which our travellers arrive – the outcomes, impact and new places, both anticipated or unexpected, which are derived through the course of their research voyages. As Rebecca Kitchen's narrative illustrates in Chapter 10, the impact of a professional doctorate can take unexpected directions and, during the course of her studies, this impact took the form of a change in role and professional setting. Rebecca also talks about the intended outcomes of her research and reflects on how far she could be in control of the 'stone' of her research, determining where it would land and how the 'ripples' and 'splashes' of impact (referred to in Chapter 9) might operate within her own professional context in educational practice. Similarly, in Chapter 8, Denise Whalley's research led to a dramatic shift in her perspective, resulting in her resignation from her position as Chair of Governors in a school. Whilst she had set out to "explore leadership literature" and to "improve my own outcome-based practice", the ideas she engaged with during the course about the nature of power and social relationships had led to a fundamental challenge to her professional identity. Simon Dowling's research, on the other hand, sought to generate ripples of impact within three domains – his own professional setting, the policy-making arena and academic theory– using a range of dissemination activities including discussion with and reporting to colleagues, academic publications, conference presentations and social media (Chapter 4).

As Hofmann argues in Chapter 11, researching one's own professional practice can be transformative through its capacity to question our taken-for-granted assumptions and habitual ways of seeing and doing things, and for some professional doctorate students the tensions and vulnerabilities are likely to result in changes in direction that will lead to and arrive at destinations far distant from those they had set out for at the point of embarkation. Bourdieu's theoretical framework, referred to in Chapter 1, draws attention to the tensions arising from working in different fields: as our voyagers' stories have shown, the consequent contradictions, vulnerabilities and dissonance in stepping outside one's habitus gives rise to an unsettling feeling of being 'at sea' but can also release the bonds of habit and fixated thinking which obstruct creativity and transformative potential.

CONCLUDING COMMENTS

This book contains the travelers' tales from one particular programme in one particular setting and context and we, as authors and editors, acknowledge that the ideas contained within these chapters cannot offer fully generalizable conclusions. However, like all maps, they tell us something about the landscapes and seas they represent and offer directions and ideas for our travelling and exploration in the future. One idea which has emerged from our mapping is that the transformative potential of professional doctorate programmes may lie in their capacity to act as crucibles for creating knowledge through a *critically inspired phronesis* (Kreber, 2015) in which traditional enclaves of professional/academic, pure/applied, theory/practice may become broken down and reconstituted as something new, emancipatory and transformative (Habermas, 1971). As our narratives have shown, these research journeys have raised questions for our researching practitioners that go beyond the straightforward problem-solving and pragmatic agendas that may have initially prompted them to engage in doctorate research and have lead our intrepid voyagers into the deeper waters where questions of values come to the surface. As Kreber argues, critically inspired phronesis – the disposition or stance of "practical wisdom" coupled with a critical perspective – offers a new vista where:

> The key questions...include: 'what values underpin what we are doing?', 'why do we think these are important?', 'are our actions consistent with these

values?', 'how have these values, these norms, and these traditions developed?', 'what injustices, harm or unsustainability do they promote?', 'who gains, who loses as a result of what we do, and by what sources of power?' And 'what can we do about this?' (2015, p. 574)

These types of question emerge in differing forms throughout our narratives and responses to them are still evolving in each case. As editors, we now invite you, the reader, to reflect on your own experience of research and of being a doctoral student or educator and to share and engage with our particular synthesis of why professional doctorate research practice is transformative.

CLOSING REFLECTIONS

From the moment I became involved in the Educational Doctorate programme on being invited to contribute a Keynote Address to the Conference at the Faculty of Education in Cambridge in June 2015, it has been an inspirational, life-changing experience. I feel as if I have become a fellow traveler with these student voyagers and their educators (though more perhaps as a passenger than fully-fledged crew member) and it has been an immense privilege to work with, and learn from, this extraordinary community. My own taken-for-granted assumptions and ideas, shaped over the course of 24 years in academic research in the field of education, have been taken apart and questioned, resulting in an authentically transformative experience for me personally and professionally. Having been exposed to diverse ways of thinking about, and doing, research, and shifted from the comfort zone of my habitus to explore the values, purposes and impact of my own research, I feel as if I have also arrived at a new place.

REFERENCES

Csikzentmihalyi, M. (1990). *Flow: The psychology of optimal experience.* New York, NY: Harper and Row.
Habermas, J. (1971). *Knowledge and human interests.* London: Heinemann.
Kreber, C. (2015). Reviving the ancient virtues in the scholarship of teaching, with a slight critical twist. *Higher Education Research and Development, 34*(3), 568–580. doi:10.1080/07294360.2014.973384
Segalas Coral, J. S., & Tejedor Papell, G. T. (2016). The role of transdisciplinarity in research and education for sustainable development. In W. Lambrechts & J. Hindson (Eds.), *Research and innovation for sustainable development.* Vienna, Austria: European Commission.

ABOUT THE CONTRIBUTORS

Julie Alderton is a University Lecturer in mathematics education at the Faculty of Education, University of Cambridge, UK. She explored the experiences of her own initial teacher education students as the focus for her Professional Doctorate. Her primary research interests are initial teacher education, gender and mathematics and reflexive research methodologies.

Pam Burnard is Professor of Arts, Creativities and Education at the Faculty of Education, University of Cambridge, UK. She holds degrees in Music Performance, Music Education, Education and Philosophy. Her primary interest is diverse creativities research, including creative teaching and learning, for which she is internationally recognised. She is the EdD programme manager at the Faculty of Education.

Tatjana Dragovic is a doctoral educator and a leader of the Leadership, Educational Improvement and Development (LEID) research community at the Faculty of Education, University of Cambridge, UK. For the last 23 years she has worked across different disciplines, sectors and industries and is recognized as an international educator, whose interdisciplinary expertise and research interests lie in the fields of creativity, leadership development, coaching, and the professional and personal development of educators.

Simon Dowling is a subject leader in a secondary school in the east of England; he has taught for a total of 23 years in several schools. He is presently in the 3rd year of the Doctorate of Education at the Faculty of Education, University of Cambridge, UK. His doctoral project investigates the influence of a newly-formed Teaching School alliance on serving teachers' professional development. His research interests include: educational leadership; collaboration for system improvement between teachers and between schools; and the challenges of securing effective professional development for classroom teachers. He has recently been appointed to lead research and development in his own school.

Julia Flutter is a Director of The Cambridge Primary Review Trust, Research Associate and postgraduate educator at the Faculty of Education, University of Cambridge. Her work on student voice is internationally recognized and she was a contributing author to 'Children, Their World, Their Education: Final Report and Recommendations of the Cambridge Primary Review' (Edited by Robin Alexander, 2009), which was awarded First Prize in the Society of Educational Studies Book Awards 2011.

Riikka Hofmann is a University Lecturer at the Faculty of Education, University of Cambridge, UK. Her research focuses on teaching, learning and leadership in educational and medical settings. She has led Masters and Doctoral research methods programmes in the Faculty and advises various UK government ministries on policy evaluations.

Rebecca Kitchen is Secondary Curriculum Leader at the Geographical Association, having formerly been a teacher and Head of Geography for 16 years. She holds degrees in Geography and Education and is a Chartered Geographer and Fellow of the Royal Geographical Society. Currently in her fourth year of the EdD programme at the Faculty of Education, University of Cambridge, UK, she is particularly interested in researching students' perceptions of geography.

James Edward Knowles leads a course called 'Access to Medicine and Dentistry', teaching Science and Mathematics at a Further Education (FE) College in the UK. Having taught for 18 years, 12 in Secondary Education and 6 in FE, he holds a BEng from Birmingham University (1996), a PGCE from Oxford University (1998) and an MA(Ed) from the Open University (2004). In his 5th year of the Doctorate of Education (EdD) at the Faculty of Education, University of Cambridge, UK, James's research interests are in how 'the self' becomes constituted through discourse and how power operates to position, enable and constrain people through their social interactions.

Wai Mun Lim is Associate Professor of Service Management at the School of Tourism and Hospitality, Plymouth University, UK. She holds degrees in Economics, Sociology and Business Management and is presently in her 1st year of the Doctorate of Education at the Faculty of Education, University of Cambridge, UK. Wai Mun's research focuses on exploring the value of international partnerships in Higher Education. Her primary interests are value co-creation in education and technological innovation and adoption.

Karen Ottewell is the Director of Academic Development & Training for International Students at the Language Centre, University of Cambridge, UK. She holds three degrees in German Language and Literature and is presently in her 1st year of the Doctorate of Education at the Faculty of Education, University of Cambridge, UK. Karen's research interest is in the development of written academic literacy. Her primary interests are assessment design, contrastive rhetoric, and the cultural influence on writing.

Gavin Turner is a subject teacher and Head of Department in a secondary school in Oxfordshire. He is in the 1st year of the Doctorate of Education at the Faculty of Education, University of Cambridge. His research focuses on self-regulation and his primary interests are motivation beliefs, specifically self-efficacy and goal orientation.

Denise Whalley taught for 25 years in a variety of East London schools whilst concurrently acting as a School Governor. She holds degrees in Science and in Leadership for Learning, and accreditations in Special Educational Needs, Reading Recovery and Chairing Governing Boards. Denise is presently in her 2nd year of the Doctorate of Education at the Faculty of Education, University of Cambridge, UK, researching the implementation of English educational policy on school governance. Her primary interests are strategic school leadership and the exercise of power within dialogic spaces.

Lightning Source UK Ltd.
Milton Keynes UK
UKOW06f0019030616

275516UK00001B/76/P